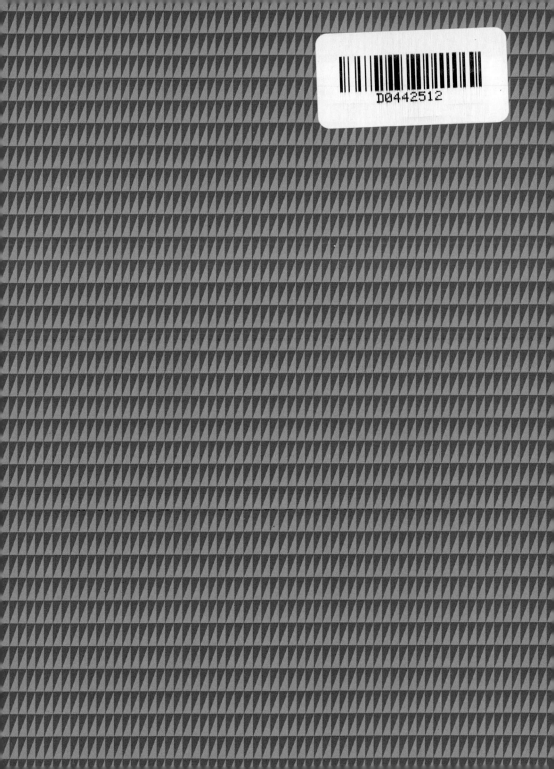

WHAT'S NEXT?

WHAT'S NEXT?

Follow Your Passion and Find Your Dream Job

—| KERRY HANNON |—

CHRONICLE BOOKS
SAN FRANCISCO

Portions of this material originally appeared in *U.S. News & World Report*.
Reprinted with permission.

Library of Congress Cataloging-in-Publication Data:
Hannon, Kerry.
What's next? : follow your passion and find your dream job / Kerry Hannon.
    p. cm.
ISBN 978-0-8118-7115-0 (hc)
1. Career changes.   2. Career development.   I. Title.
HF5384.H364 2010
650.14—dc22
                    2009048584

Manufactured in China.

Designed by Supriya Kalidas.
Typeset in Gotham, Garamond Premier Pro.

10 9 8 7 6 5 4 3 2 1

Chronicle Books LLC
680 Second Street
San Francisco, California 94107

www.chroniclebooks.com

TO MY SISTER, PAT BONNEY, AND
MY HUSBAND, CLIFF, WITH GRATITUDE

CONTENTS

When I met the late John Gardner in 1995, he was in his eighties, and going strong. Although hardly a household name today, Gardner had served with distinction as Secretary of Health, Education, and Welfare during Lyndon Johnson's administration. He created the prestigious White House Fellows program. He founded Common Cause, the first significant campaign finance reform organization, and Independent Sector, a forum that provides a voice for the nonprofit world. A few years later he would help launch Civic Ventures and Experience Corps in order to mobilize others in their second half of life to create a better world. There were many other ventures in between, along with a string of influential books on leadership, community, and self-renewal.

What I did not realize at the time is that he achieved all this after the age of fifty. For Gardner, the gold watch turned out to be a launch pad—the beginning of a new chapter that comprised his most significant achievements.

He is hardly the only person to claim such a trajectory. There are many other high-flyers who have gone from success to even greater significance. Former United States President Jimmy Carter created a more enduring legacy after his presidency. Al Gore's encore career earned him the Nobel Peace Prize. And when Bill Gates departed Microsoft he emphasized that he wasn't retiring. In his words, he was "reordering priorities," concentrating on the most important challenges he could imagine—ending poverty, curing disease, educating all.

As examples of these vaunted second acts proliferate, Kerry Hannon's wonderful and enlightening book, *What's Next?*, offers hope and help to the rest of us. It is a compelling reminder that the chapters stretching beyond Act I are something to look forward to—a time of new meaning, immense contribution, and continued income.

By addressing the genuine challenges of what continues to be, for many, a do-it-yourself transition, this book proves that the midlife shift to new fulfillment is not only possible, but deeply desirable. It offers a set of compelling, credible role models, and distills their insights and experiences into a reliable roadmap for successfully planning this transition. What's more, as *What's Next?* shows us, these uplifting encore opportunities are hardly exclusive to former CEOs and Commanders-in-Chief. They are within reach for anyone.

As you ponder what you will do for your encore, remember that you're in good company. Tens of millions of Americans are celebrating their fiftieth and sixtieth birthdays, making the shift from "what's last?" to "what's next?" more than a question of personal fulfillment. What millions will do next is a matter of national importance. How will we, as a nation, make the most of this talent and experience? How will we make it easier for the largest, best-educated, healthiest, and longest-living generations to create a better world for the generations that follow?

What's Next? starts the conversation by redefining success. I hope you start there, too. Then read this book for the encouragement, guidance, and tools to make your dreams—and the dreams of those you can help in your encore career—come true.

MARC FREEDMAN *Founder/CEO, Civic Ventures*

INTRODUCTION

A New York investment banker becomes a small-town chef. A college professor becomes a chocolatier. An entrenched corporate exec accepts an early-retirement package and converts to the ministry.

Who doesn't fantasize about a second career?

Perhaps you've worked in the same field for twenty-some-odd years and have run out of fresh challenges. Maybe you feel you have talents that are going to waste. Or there's something you've always wanted to do that's calling louder and louder. Or, like millions of others, you're simply worn down by the corporate routine. There must be something out there that's more meaningful and more rewarding, right?

As many as 8.4 million Americans between the ages of forty-four and seventy have already launched "encore careers," positions that combine income with personal meaning and social impact, according to a recent survey on boomers, work, and aging by the MetLife Foundation and Civic Ventures, a San Francisco nonprofit organization dedicated to expanding the contribution of older Americans to society. Of those workers surveyed who are not already in second careers, half are interested in them.

"Very few people start a second career purely for the money," says Marc Freedman, founder and CEO of Civic Ventures. "They're searching for work that is fulfilling and gets them out of bed in the morning." While these work transitions involve following a dream or a calling, you don't want to get caught up in the romance of it all. "There is a blitheness that all you have to do is embrace your passion and the rest happens magically," Freedman warns. "It's not that easy. You don't open the doors to your bed-and-breakfast and the cheering crowds arrive."

For more than three years, I have written a highly successful feature for *U.S. News & World Report* called "Second Acts" in which I profile a person who has made such a move. I cheerfully refer to it as happy journalism and have been fortunate to fly around the country meeting people from all walks of life, ranging in age from early forties to seventy-plus, who have taken up a new course. Each one followed his or her own heart down a new path with single-mindedness, passion, humbleness, and an ability to live moderately.

After forty, it can be daunting to start a second act. The mere thought of going back to school, learning new skills, or starting over at the bottom of the ladder stops many people from trying something new. In turbulent economic times, making a major move is more daunting than ever.

Sally forth. These times, in fact, may demand it. If you have lost a job, have accepted an early-retirement package, or are a retiree or soon-to-be retiree facing significantly smaller retirement accounts (and need to keep working longer than you had planned while the stock market recovers), it's your moment.

Use your turn of events as an unexpected opportunity to reinvent your own career or to pursue a long-held dream. You may never have a better chance, or reason, to do so—to get excited about work once again, to feel revived and passionate about making a difference in the world. Your new career could easily outlast your first one.

If the prospect presents itself, reach for something totally new. Seize the silver lining. Try a new path. This is your time.

A TOUGH COP TURNED NASHVILLE MUSIC AGENT

▼

To be the toughest female cop alive, you have to run three miles uphill, climb three hundred stairs, put the shot, climb ropes, bench-press, run a hundred-meter sprint, swim one hundred meters, and complete an obstacle course three football fields in length—eight events in one day.

Jill Angel has done that. And won. In 1988 and 1992 she captured the state of California "Toughest Cop Alive" endurance competition for women and came in second in the worldwide event in 1989.

Don't be fooled by her five-foot-three, 120-pound physique. She's tenacious—and strong. For twenty-two years, Angel, fifty-three, was a California Highway Patrol (CHP) officer, rising through the ranks from sergeant to assistant chief in Los Angeles, overseeing more than a thousand officers. It was a job she prized, and for a while, she was unstoppable. She witnessed the aftermath of countless horrendous traffic fatalities and was severely beaten by a drug-addled suspect. Afterward, as head of the CHP's Critical Incident Response Team, she passed out at a shooting scene—partly from exhaustion.

Then it all fell apart. Handling nothing but the worst stuff on the Critical Incident Response Team for five years had taken its toll.

Physically, she was spent: she had high blood pressure, migraine headaches, depression, and an inability to sleep soundly.

A single mom with two young daughters, now ten and thirteen, Angel realized it was time to make a change. She handed in her badge and retired. But it was the power of music that really helped her turn the corner. And now she's in training to be the toughest music agent alive.

Angel has dabbled in the music business since 2003. It began on a whim, trying to help a coworker get her music heard in Nashville, where Angel had a younger cousin, Ilene, an aspiring songwriter. While still on duty, she began making monthly trips to Nashville, landing meetings with the heads of record labels and top producers. "Being an assistant chief at the time, I was determined to get through to people at my level. They didn't know what to do with me," she recalls. But she scored her ten-minute face time, and it made a lasting impression.

"People told me I would meet the worst people in the music business. 'They lie to you' and so on, they cautioned," Angel says. "I said, 'Are you kidding? I just spent twenty-two years as a police officer and was a commander in South Central Los Angeles. The music people are some of the nicest people I've met.'"

While her fellow staffer never did land a record deal, Angel fell in love with Nashville and her cousin's music. "The more I listened to Ilene's songs, the more I believed in her talent. They gave me hope, especially in the dark days after I retired." She began pitching her cousin's work with a vengeance.

For Angel, it wasn't a big jump from serving as a CHP officer to pursuing the music business full time. "Both are making the world better somehow, though the two fields couldn't be more different in how they go about doing it," she says. And she can afford to be patient. Angel and her family can live on her CHP pension, which provides full health benefits.

Since moving into her new gig managing singers and song-writers, Angel has worked with a half-dozen artists, but her biggest success to date is her cousin. Ilene's song "I Don't Think About It," sung by Emily Osment, costar of the TV show *Hannah Montana*, hit the Radio Disney Top 10, where it stayed for over four months. It went to No. 1 for three straight weeks.

Moreover, Nashville artists, including Dolly Parton, Tim McGraw, Reba McEntire, Wynonna Judd, LeAnn Rimes, and Kenny Rogers, have put "holds" on several of Ilene's songs, expressing interest in recording them. Another protégé, Angel's nephew Matthew, nineteen, a Los Angeles–based actor and singer/songwriter, has finished his first album, and his acting career has taken off.

Angel called her mentor, Dick Whitehouse, a former record-label head who has advised her for four years, to tell him she and Ilene were No. 1 on Disney with Ilene's song. His response: "Of course you are. You're Jill."

And that's why she just might become the toughest agent in Nashville.

— Q&A —

LOOKING BACK

K.H. / **What did the transition mean to you personally?**

J.A. / What drove me was wanting as many people as possible to heal with the music I was healing with at the time. My law-enforcement career had ended. Twenty-two years of law enforcement and I was really sick—completely stressed out. Multiple fatalities, line of duty deaths . . . after years of that I was depressed.

At the time, music was really therapeutic to me. I started listening to Ilene's songs. I threw myself into songs being written by her and a couple of her songwriting friends. I found myself healing with their music.

K.H. / **Were you confident that you were doing the right thing? Any second-guessing?**

J.A. / I was totally confident. I actually craved trying to make Ilene happen.

K.H. / **Anything you would have done differently?**

J.A. / I would have been more selective about how I invested the money. I spent everything I had and at the same time went through a divorce that finished me off financially. So here I am six years later and very selective about how I put money into this.

You have to know where to spend the money and where not to. I learned all of that the hard way. It really does take firsthand experience and listening to other people. I didn't listen hard enough because I didn't trust most people in the business. I was so driven to make it happen myself. I was so confident. I actually thought I could make it in three months.

You can spend $1,000 recording one song demo, and everything my clients wrote I was having demoed if I liked it. There were also the costs of traveling back and forth to Nashville from California. And if someone said they would listen to a song, I would overnight it. A month later I'd be in that producer's office, and I would see my envelope in the corner on the floor with all the other piles of stuff not even opened.

I spent so much money. I didn't know once we had a number one song that it wouldn't bring in enough money to make this thing really take off. If I knew years ago what I know today, I would have a ton more money. Do I regret any of it? Absolutely not! I feel like I'm just beginning.

K.H. / **How do you measure your success?**

J.A. / There's so much soul-searching. How do we measure success? There has been a huge success with each person I have worked with, but the success and rewards have not been financial for me. Helping people make a living singing at gigs four nights a week—maybe not a record deal, but doing what they love and sharing their gift—that's an achievement. I did make some money off Ilene's number one song. Truthfully, at this point, I haven't made nearly what I have put into it. It has mostly been emotional rewards. I don't know how I can stop doing this, so hopefully the money will follow.

K.H. / **How big a role did financial rewards play in your decision to make a transition?**

J.A. / None whatsoever. My goal was that I wanted my clients to have financial security. Very few artists get rewarded for their gifts. Not that I don't want to make money. I do. A fixed income at my age isn't really enough with young children. So I took a standard cut for my kids' college tuition. But I was not driven by money. If I stay with my fixed income in retirement and pay attention to spending, I'll be okay.

K.H. / **How did your preparation help you succeed?**

J.A. / There were several things that helped get me started and keep me going:

First, I found a mentor whom I can ask questions and bounce ideas off of, and who can open doors for me sometimes.

Second, I got my kids excited about it, so I have that support at home. They love it. I take them whenever I can. They love being in the studio. Now they are in performing arts schools. One takes voice lessons. One takes guitar lessons. All this came out of my pursuing this endeavor. Neither one of them had any interest until I started doing this.

Third, I was confident. I may have overdone it, at least initially. I just jumped. And I learned as I went. It has kind of been that way my whole life. In the past, doors have opened for me. I learned not to be afraid to run through them. I've always been able to make things happen for myself. I looked at this the same way. At the time, I was wrong because everything I didn't learn before cost me financially.

What I didn't know about it also helped me. I didn't know that things that were happening for me don't usually happen. I'm so glad I didn't know that. There are thirty thousand songwriters in Nashville, and here I was taking Ilene's songs directly to heads of record labels. These were people I shouldn't have been able to get a meeting with, but I just called them, and they met with me. It has taken time, but those contacts are beginning to make things happen now and will continue to in the future. I'm convinced.

▲

"You have to know where to spend the money and where not to. I learned all of that the hard way. It really does take firsthand experience and listening to other people. I didn't listen hard enough because I didn't trust most people in the business. I was so driven to make it happen myself."

▼

K.H. / **What do you tell other people who ask for your advice?**
J.A. / You have to have dreams or passions. You have to be willing to take huge risks to make big things happen. You also have to be sure of

yourself and open to unexpected opportunities. It's not easy to out-last the challenges of starting something new. I spent the last five or six years throwing myself into this thing, and it is a very tough, tough business.

The business took off at first, then boom—I hit a wall. I almost gave up, and then this hot up-and-coming band called Tennessee Hollow came along. They wanted me to represent them. I heard their music, and I thought, I can't take on a band right now. I want to be done with being an agent. I have pretty much invested everything I have. I'm out of money!

But I had faith. I agreed to spend two days in Nashville and con-nect them to everybody I know. Some of the producers were heads of record labels! They were the "huge" people who took me five years to reach—and everybody I called took a meeting. It was forty-eight hours of the most effortless work I've ever known in my life. One day we were even at the home of the head of Sugar Hill Records. I had sent him a link and told him I really wanted him to check out the band. It was an experience right out of a movie.

By the end of it, I had three record labels interested and a show-case performing live. Two labels challenged me to book a hundred gigs and develop a fan base over the next year. I signed a one-year con-tract with Tennessee Hollow and booked them as the opening act for a major Sugar Hill Records artist. My goal is to launch them in a year.

K.H. / **What books or resources did you use or recommend others to use?**
J.A. / A book will get you started, but it won't tell you how to connect with people. You need to experience things. Producers would take a meeting with me, and we always had a great time. Martina McBride's producer and I spent forty-five minutes talking about motorcycles—Harleys versus BMWs. He wanted to know why CHPs rode BMWs. The thing I love the most in life is connecting with people—and they remember me.

K.H. / **What are some of the unexpected rewards and surprises?**

J.A. / One of the songs I recorded saved someone's life. It's called "Time to Fly," written by my cousin Ilene. A colleague from the California Highway Patrol was suicidal. She bought the CD and played it all the time—and eventually decided not to take her life. If you listen to the song and the words, you will see why. I spent six years and every penny I had, throwing heart and soul into that album. If all that was about one person hearing that one song that one time, it was all worth it.

BUILDING A NETWORK AND PREPARING
FOR SETBACKS

FIND A MENTOR. Who do you know who might be able to guide you along your new path? Take the time to meet with your mentor and enlist his or her invaluable help behind the scenes in learning the ropes. Delve into your network of friends, family, and business colleagues. Tap into LinkedIn and Facebook contacts. If you're interested in starting a small business, check out StartupNation.com, a site dedicated to small-business groups.

BROADEN YOUR MENTOR SEARCH. Get involved in your local Rotary Club and contact the chamber of commerce near you. Another way to connect with a reliable person to guide you is through SCORE (www.score.org), a nonprofit association dedicated to educating entrepreneurs and to the formation, growth, and success of small businesses nationwide. SCORE is a resource partner with the U.S. Small Business Administration (SBA). The organization, founded in 1954, is headquartered in Herndon, Virginia, and Washington, D.C., and has 370 chapters throughout the United States and its territories, with roughly twelve thousand mentors nationwide. Both working and retired executives and business owners donate time and expertise as business counselors. SCORE mentors will advise you for free, in person or online. The Association of Small Business Development Centers (www.asbdc-us.org), a joint effort of the SBA universities, colleges, and local governments, provides no-cost consulting and low-cost training at about a thousand locations.

PRIME YOUR SALES PITCH. Evaluate your skill set and be confident. If cold calling isn't your top move, focus on your best sales technique and hone it to market your new venture.

BE PREPARED FOR SETBACKS. Starting a new business in uncharted territory takes time. It might take off like gangbusters, but in time, you will hit the inevitable setbacks. This not only will require internal fortitude, but also will force you to ask others for help and guidance. This is when a solid mentor by your side comes in handy.

SEEK AND LISTEN TO ADVICE FROM PEOPLE WHO HAVE BEEN SUCCESSFUL IN THE FIELD. They can help you find leads when you're ready to get your foot in the door, but more important, they can give you a real sense of what their work is like on a day-to-day basis. Use their advice to get a sense of what has worked for them in the past and what stumbling blocks to avoid, as well as a sense of what the work entails and what opportunities might be out there for someone with your background.

TAP INTO YOUR PERSONAL NETWORK. You never know who can bring you clients or help you build your business. Reach out to potential contacts through alumni publications, Web sites, or regional associations, if there's a chapter near you.

ASK FOR HELP IN STAGES. Don't be vague and simply ask someone to be your mentor. It's better to clearly ask for a small, easily delivered act of kindness, and once he or she has done so, your mentor may continue to be interested in helping you the next time. Let the relationship evolve organically step-by-step.

MEET PEOPLE. You are more likely to identify likely mentors if you seek out groups and activities that will allow you to meet new people. Explore nonprofit work that will allow you to show what you can do, and build working relationships with a whole new cast of potential mentors.

DON'T BE DEFENSIVE. When you ask for pointers, be prepared to listen carefully and put your emotional reactions aside. That's what a critique is all about—improvement.

SAY "THANKS." Write thank-you notes and look for other simple ways to express your appreciation when someone goes out of his or her way to support you. It works wonders in building relationships.

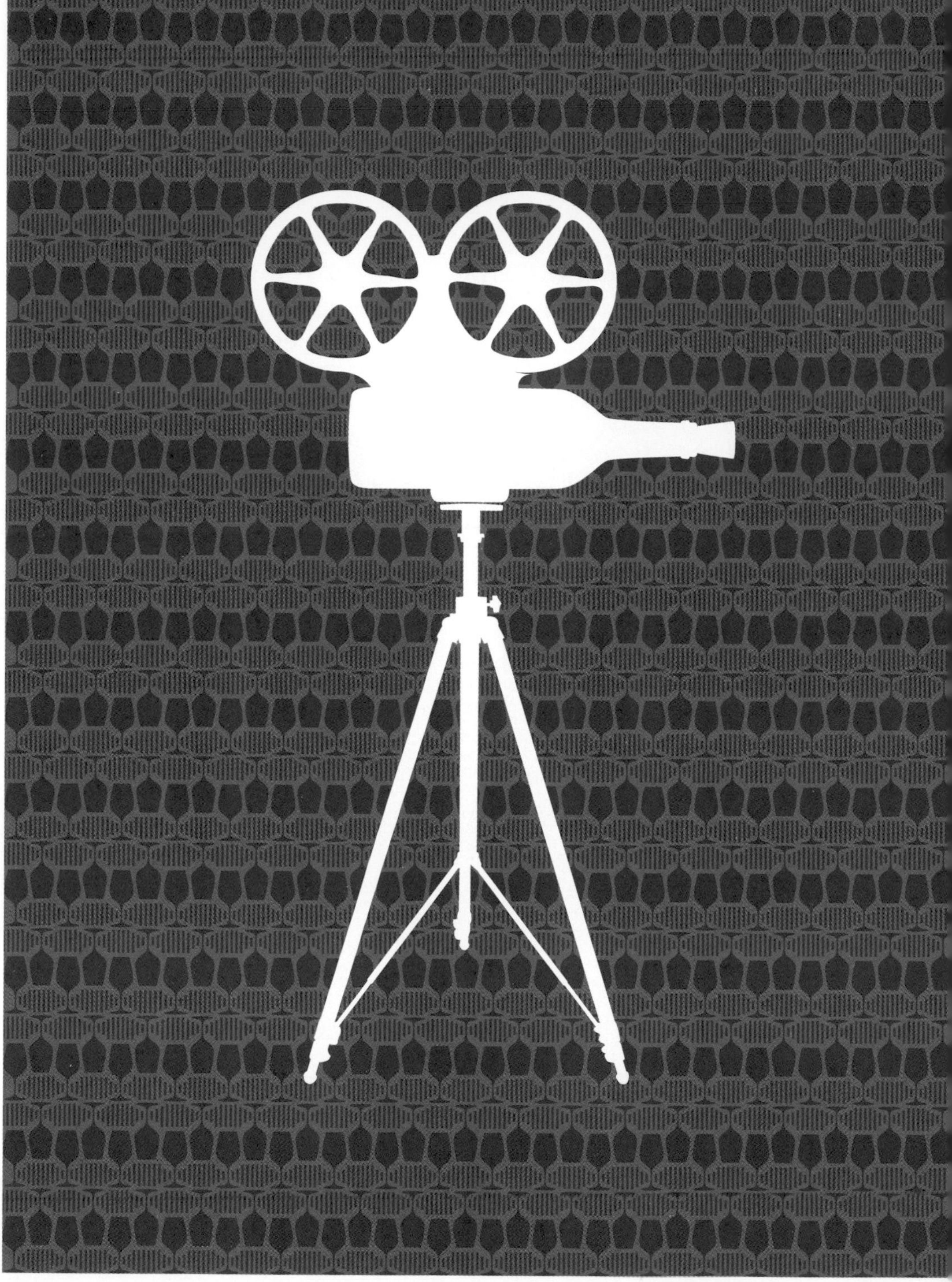

A CROSS-COUNTRY JOURNEY FROM NEWS TO WINE

Becoming a winemaker—never mind a winemaker in Walla Walla, Washington—had never crossed Steve Brooks's mind. Then he stumbled upon a *New York Times* story about the fast-growing wine industry in the tiny verdant town near the Blue Mountains.

That chance reading came at an opportune time. Brooks, then a veteran TV producer at CNN in Atlanta, was growing disillusioned with the gloom of the news business and the strains of his perpetual travel schedule. At the end of 2001, after a nineteen-year career at the cable network, Brooks, at the age of forty, took a buyout. He had met his wife, Lori, at CNN and traveled the world covering news stories. "The finest part of those typically long days in the field was enjoying the local wine and trading stories with colleagues," Brooks recalls.

The article sparked a yearning to make a change in his life and his family's. "I missed spending time with my wife and two daughters, then ages two and seven. In the back of my head, I knew I had to find something else to do. I didn't want to stay there for another twenty years and be grumpy and unhappy," he says.

Brooks had never before made wine or even studied wine-making. "Plus, I thought only multimillionaires could afford to own a winery," he says. Living in a town like Walla Walla, with thirty thousand residents in the remote southeastern corner of Washington State, was further from his mind. He had never even heard of it. But after talking the scheme over with his wife, Brooks told everyone he knew that he was going to start his own winery. "That way, I couldn't back out of it," he says with a laugh. "At CNN, I was always confident that I could do as good a job as anyone else," he adds. "Why couldn't I take that faith in myself to another career? Every other winemaker in the world started out at the same spot . . . knowing nothing."

So the couple quit their high-paying jobs, sold the family home, packed the kids into their Volvo wagon, and headed to the Pacific Northwest to start anew in a town where they knew nary a soul. Brooks enrolled in the local community college's Center for Enology and Viticulture for the hands-on study of every stage of winemaking, from planting the vines to harvesting, fermenting, and bottling. He also worked as an apprentice to top-drawer winemakers in the region.

Finally, in 2005 he began to make his own wine, buying grapes from established Washington State vineyards. "I couldn't afford to buy land and still can't," he says. "That's a gigantic investment. It's not like growing carrots." Instead, Brooks finds the best fruit to buy and determines when the grapes are ready to be picked. Vineyard laborers harvest the grapes, and Brooks hauls them back to a leased building outfitted with top-of-the-line equipment to work his magic.

Brooks is a one-man shop. But he's quick to ask the advice of veteran vintners. "People here are very sharing of their information," he says. "I wanted to make a rosé. I called up a winemaker I admired and said, 'If I buy you lunch, can you tell me how you did it?'" He did.

"For the first Syrah blend I put together, I changed my mind so many times it was silly," he says. "I asked a friend who has made plenty of well-received wines for his opinion—at least three times. Then, at the last second, I did what my gut told me to do and didn't listen to anyone else. The Syrah got ninety points [out of a hundred from a respected wine reviewer]."

In 2009, the winery's production is expected to rise to 1,500 cases—triple that of three years ago. Retail prices range from $16 for a rosé of Cabernet Franc to $40 for a half bottle of Sémillon ice wine. Brooks's wines are sold in roughly 125 outlets in Washington, Oregon, Idaho, and Georgia. Later this year, he is starting online sales through Amazon.com and the winery's own site, www.trustcellars.com.

For now, Brooks pours all revenues back into the growing business, while Lori's income as a freelance TV sports director keeps the family afloat until the winery begins to turn a profit. And Brooks exudes a laid-back confidence that it will: "I feel like I will never ever know everything there is to know . . . but I have a good product, thanks to the training I had from winemakers at the top of their profession."

Trust is what his journey from news producer to winemaker is about, and it's also the name of his winery: Trust Cellars. And he shares that philosophy with his customers in a message on his wine bottle labels: "To change, to shift. To make an about-face. To move from a lifestyle rooted in technology and speed to an existence focusing on soil and sun. Taking a giant step requires trust. The trust of your family and friends . . . and the trust in yourself."

— Q & A —
LOOKING BACK

K.H. / **What did the transition mean to you personally?**
S.B. / It wasn't a touchy-feely thing. I just knew that I wanted to do

something else before I died—I was bored with what I was doing, and there had to be something else out there that was more fulfilling.

In television, even though the on-screen correspondents get all the praise, in reality forty or fifty people are behind them doing everything. I wanted to do something that was just me, where everything wasn't a group decision. There were so many things I felt got watered down to the point where they weren't very exciting ideas anymore. I wanted to try something that was all mine—either good or bad—I was the one responsible for it.

"I was always confident that I could do as good a job as anyone else. Why couldn't I take that faith in myself to another career?"

K.H. / **Were you confident in what you were doing? Did you second-guess yourself at all along the way?**

S.B. / There are times when I second-guessed whether it was really possible to make a living. And sometimes I still think, wow, am I really ever going to get big enough to provide for everybody? It takes patience or plenty of up-front capital. If I'd started with a lot of money, I'd be better off, no doubt.

But even with money, I'd still have to build the brand name and reputation. Since I'm not a stock car driver or a golfer with name recognition, I wasn't going to release twenty thousand cases of wine and expect to sell it all in a year's time as I needed to. I had to start smallish and build and build and build.

K.H. / **Is there anything you would have done differently?**

S.B. / There are little things, but to be honest, not really. I wish I had saved up more money and started with more capital. It is not safe and easy to head off on your own. And I missed those benefits and that paycheck every two weeks. But I would do it again, that's for sure. I'm pretty happy with how things unfolded.

K.H. / **Have there been any big surprises or unexpected rewards?**

S.B. / I have certainly met a lot of people who are very fun and very cool. That is really the best part of it—hanging out in the tasting room all weekend and meeting people from all over the country. It is not something I ever really thought about ahead of time. And I have gotten some really good reviews that I didn't think I would get this early.

K.H. / **Is spending more time with family a bonus?**

S.B. / Well, that was originally part of the idea! Right now I work more than I did before—way more. I honestly didn't think that was possible. I very rarely take weekends off. During harvest it can be twelve to sixteen hours a day, seven days a week for six to eight weeks. The rest of the year it seems to be usually eight- or ten-hour days, but that's still seven days a week. I'm not complaining at all, though—for me, even the longest day at the winery is far better than the shortest day before at CNN.

K.H. / **How big a role did potential financial rewards play in your decision?**

S.B. / Money was not a motivator for me. It helped, of course, that Lori was still pulling in a good income from her freelance work as a TV sports director. Having a partner to share the financial load during these start-up years is an important piece of why I am able to take on this second act.

K.H. / **How did your preparation help you succeed?**

S.B. / You have to get your family on board with your dream. You can't do it otherwise. Especially for something as drastic as moving across the country. Our kids weren't crazy about it, but they are glad now.

Second, I didn't just say I was going to start a winery and—boom—it was off and running. It took a few years to get here. I left CNN at the end of 2001, and we got out here in 2003. During those years we were spending a lot of time looking at property, trying to figure out where to go.

The best part was that once I got here, I was able to learn first-hand what the job was all about by working for other wineries and vineyards. That was the best training. I actually got paid at some of them, although it was minimum wage. I was a cellar rat, and I did that for three years off and on. During that time, I was putting my business plan in place. I took pertinent classes—the science of winemaking and vineyard management at the local community college's Center for Enology and Viticulture.

K.H. / **What do you tell people who come to you for advice on starting a second act?**

S.B. / I tell them to first find out what it is really like. Specifically to winemaking, people think it is glamorous and it's awesome and all you do is sit around and drink wine all day. Like many other jobs, that's not the reality, and it's important for people to know. Take a "work-cation." Working vacations let you set up for a few days at a winery, a B&B, or something that you think you really want to do. You find out what it is like working at those jobs even if it's for a brief time. Chances are the reality is nothing as enchanting as what it seems.

K.H. / **How do you measure your success at this point?**

S.B. / I figure there are two things you can look at—sales and reviews. They don't always equate. Reviews are all over the place. I have submitted the same wine and gotten everything from great reviews to "not recommended." A better measure for me is sales. People talk with their wallets. If you can sell wine to people in the tasting room where they're tasting it, that's good. Last year our profit was up pretty close to threefold. Still not huge numbers, but I can tell it is going in the right direction.

AN ALTERNATIVE GETAWAY

Want to find out if that dream job is so dreamy?

Brian Kurth can help. In 2004 he founded VocationVacations (www.vocationvacations.com). Based in Portland, Oregon, the company lets you get a taste of what it might be like to be a butcher, baker, or candlestick maker, and much more.

The idea is straightforward: take your dream job and do it (without quitting your day job). The hands-on training trips, lasting up to three days, are conducted under the guidance of expert mentors who are typically small- and medium-size-business owners and operators, both for-profit and nonprofit. "It's a true career transition tool either for people who are planning for the future or for people who fear they are going to be laid off," Kurth says.

Since its inception, VocationVacations has enlisted more than four hundred career mentors in over 180 vocations across the country. Among the occupations: chef, private investigator, sports announcer, and fishing guide. Also available for sampling are a number of careers that may never have crossed your radar, for example: alpaca rancher or sword maker. Vacationers pay a fee ranging from $545 to $2,000 (airfare and lodging not included), though most pay under $1,200.

Today, 80 percent of those who sign up for a VocationVacations adventure are looking to change careers, according to Kurth. "We deal with people who are actually making career transitions, making dreams a reality. About 20 percent of our alums are now in their dream jobs."

Kurth developed the idea for VocationVacations back in 1999. "I wanted to be my own customer. I was doing the corporate grind in Chicago, working for a telecommunications company. I was burning out and daydreaming one day stuck in traffic on the Kennedy Expressway in Chicago, staring at brake lights, thinking there's got to be more to life than this."

He began to wonder what it would be like to try a new career. His three choices were to work in the wine industry, become a dog day-care owner or dog trainer, or become a tour or travel guide. The idea of forming a company that offered short-term career internships for adults to learn more about these kinds of jobs seemed like a no-brainer. But it took a pink slip nearly five years later to light the fire.

Freed from his job, Kurth spent six months traveling across America asking people in various stopping points what they did for a living, what they wish they could do, and what their job would be if they could follow their passion. He jotted their answers in a journal. That on-the-road homework gave him a working list of job categories his new firm could line up for VocationVacations.

A VocationVacation is designed as the first step in a series of moves to get to your ultimate dream job or dream business. "It's the due diligence, personal and professional, of exploring a career change without taking any risks. You're spending a couple of days, but you aren't changing your life—yet," he says. As an added bonus, your VocationVacation includes two phone sessions with a career coach. To be honest, deciding in two days to transform your career by 360 degrees is probably not going to happen. "It is a weathervane directional of telling you where do I want to go from here," Kurth says. "But if your passion hasn't dimmed when you get back from your experience, then you might begin the process to take it to the next level—budgeting for a transition, adding new skills by going back to school, and writing a business plan."

TOP TEN VOCATIONVACATIONS

ANIMATOR

BAKER

BED-AND-BREAKFAST OWNER

CHOCOLATIER

DOG DAY-CARE OWNER

FASHION BUYER/DESIGNER

BOUTIQUE HOTEL MANAGER

MUSIC PRODUCER

NONPROFIT DIRECTOR

PHOTOGRAPHER

FORM A CAREER CHANGE CLUB

JOIN FORCES WITH A GROUP OF OTHER PEOPLE WHO ARE LOOKING TO MAKE A CHANGE. They can run the gamut from being unfulfilled in their work, unemployed, or completely burned out in their current jobs. The key connection: you're all ready to discover ways to pursue your next act. In *Test-Drive Your Dream Job*, written by Brian Kurth, founder of VocationVacations, Kurth explores this process. Some tips:

- Start recruiting members by talking to your friends and coworkers. Consider posting flyers at gathering places—e.g., coffee houses, civic organizations, churches, play groups, libraries, health clubs.

- Keep it small. Suggested membership: a minimum of four and maximum of twelve.

- Set a meeting place and time.

- Topics to discuss: define a great job, and address fears such as financial instability, family disruption, giving up an identity, failing at something new—all possible stumbling blocks to a successful career transition.

- Write action plans and lists of all the things you need to learn and do in order to realize a great new job. Be accountable to each other for your accomplishments each week.

- Brainstorm about ways to find a mentor. Having a mentor is at the heart of a successful career transition.

FROM STRESS TO BLISS

When Lisa Eaves meets new patients, they inevitably ask: "Do you have kids?" And when she says no, their knee-jerk response is: "Why are you doing this?"

Eaves, fifty-two, is a licensed acupuncture therapist in Washington, D.C., who specializes in fertility and women's health issues. She's the sole proprietor of Heal From Within Acupuncture and the Mind/Body Fertility Program of D.C., a ten-week workshop. Ninety percent of her practice is treating women trying to get pregnant.

"I love children but never imagined having any of my own," she says. "It seemed like a good balance to me—not bringing any children into the world myself, I spend my time helping other people do so."

Eaves's softly lit office oozes a New Agey ambience, from the background music wafting through the space to a richly woven rug hanging on the wall, flickering candles, and a bowl of smooth stones. A very Zen-like aura lingers. It's the antithesis of her once hard-charging world as a highly ranked technical support manager at Fannie Mae, where it was not unusual for Eaves to be tied to her beeper 24/7. "I was incredibly driven. For eleven years, I was constantly in the office working," she recalls.

She was rewarded with a salary nearing six figures and all the benefits. But she burned out. "There is a price you pay for staying where you are. It kills your spirit after a while."

Eaves's spirit and approach to life have always been nontraditional—evolving over time. After high school, she barnstormed the country, playing outfield on a women's softball team. "My education was on the road," she says, laughing.

In the off-season, she pieced together college credits at the University of Louisville, close to her Kentucky childhood home. Finally, at twenty-seven, she headed east. She finished her bachelor of science degree in business at the University of Maryland in 1987 and quickly landed a job managing contracts for a firm building turnkey systems for the U.S. Department of Defense.

During that time, Eaves was diagnosed with melanoma. "It was really scary to have the big 'C,'" she recalls. She began doing meditation and looking for teachers. She went to different churches trying to find answers. With the original melanoma, they removed about 10 square inches from her back. There was no chemo or radiation. It had nothing to do with stress, she says. "I believe youthful sunbathing was the primary contributor." There have been two more bad patches since, all surgically removed without chemo or radiation.

In 1993 she accepted a position at Fannie Mae and quickly became immersed in her work. At the time, a friend was studying acupuncture. Eaves was curious about how it might help her deal with her work stress but pushed it aside—until she faced the milestone of turning forty. A two-week rafting trip through the Grand Canyon stirred things up. She spent her time off the river keeping a journal and losing herself in the beauty of the landscape and her thoughts. "It was unsettling," she recalls. "I was going to be forty. I was alone. My family was far away, and I was trying to figure out what I was doing here."

When she returned to Washington, she started reading about Chinese medicine, made acupuncture appointments for herself, visited the Maryland Institute of Traditional Chinese Medicine, and enrolled in classes. She both worked and went to school full time, but eventually she began working three days a week. In 2000, after graduation, she started a part-time practice but held on at Fannie Mae for four more years.

Financially, Eaves made it work by living simply and always putting money away. In addition, she had saved carefully before heading off on her own, built up a healthy 401(k), and accumulated a respectable amount of Fannie Mae company stock.

After five years, her practice pulls in more revenue than she was making at Fannie Mae. There are marketing expenses, rent, a book-keeper, health insurance, and her retirement fund, but she is making a better living than she was in her corporate days.

Eaves sees more than thirty patients a week, in addition to her Mind/Body workshops. "I coach these women," she says. "Acupuncture is just the tip of it. It's not just a physical treatment. You really tap into people's energy and their spirit. It's a little lightning rod to the human spirit."

In her workshops, she teaches stress-reduction techniques and ways to harness inner strength through meditation, yoga, and nutrition.

The group discusses stress hormones that are in the bloodstream when a woman is going through fertility treatment. "It's right up there with people having been diagnosed with cancer and other life-threatening diseases," Eaves says. That anxiety "challenges everything you have ever thought about yourself and your marriage, your spouse, your relationship with God, and who you are. It's a very isolating experience that brings everything to the surface. My goal is for them to be at peace, whatever the outcome is."

LOOKING BACK

K.H. / **What were you going through personally and emotionally at the time of the move?**

L.E. / I was turning forty and had taken a trip through the Grand Canyon, which really opened up my heart to possibilities. That was a milestone. And I felt unsettled at Fannie Mae every day. It just wasn't doing it for me. I was kind of surprised I was there anyway because I am not technical. I had to work so hard because things did not come easily for me. I just couldn't stay there. I had to go.

As I started taking courses, I began to look inside and answer some important questions: What am I best at? What are my gifts? Today, I know. Working with people is easy. I love it. I love starting the healing process for others.

K.H. / **Any second-guessing along the way?**

L.E. / The only time I felt uncertain was the first thirty days after I quit Fannie Mae completely. It was so scary. All the safety nets were gone. No money was going to appear magically in my checking account every two weeks. No health benefits. No stock options. But almost magically after a month, I realized, it's going to be okay; I can do this.

K.H. / **Is there anything you would have done differently?**

L.E. / I don't really know how I could have done anything differently, because I made decisions based on what I knew at the time. I took it in incremental steps: I graduated. I got my license. I started treating people part time. I ramped up my practice to full speed.

K.H. / **Any unexpected rewards? Surprises?**

L.E. / I never envisioned I'd go into fertility specialization. Now that is what I am known for. The workshops were a surprise as well. They evolved out of what I was doing with the fertility treatments, and now they are in such demand. I have been able to grow myself as a person helping others with their process in those sessions.

K.H. / **How important were financial rewards to your desire to make a change?**

L.E. / I never really thought I was going to make much money. I thought, if I could make as much money as I was making at Fannie Mae, I'd be happy. I'm actually making more, which is even better!

K.H. / **How did your preparation help you make the transition?**

L.E. / Training in advance was key. I was able to keep working full time while I went to school at night. I also did advance financial planning. Knowing that I was going to take a pay cut to quit Fannie Mae, I sold my old car early on and bought a car I knew would last a long time. I refinanced my apartment and got my mortgage payment down. Low expenses helped a lot.

K.H. / **What do you tell others who ask your advice about starting a new career?**

L.E. / I tell them to ask themselves these three questions:

- What comes naturally to me?
- How do I love to spend my time?
- What makes me feel good about myself?

I tell them to contemplate those questions over and over again. It's tough. When you ask how they love to spend their time, a lot of people say, "Well, I like to walk on the beach." Well, you can't make a living that way. You have to really sit with those questions. It's a process, and it may take years. Allow yourself to be open to exploring what comes up and then move in that direction, learn about it, and ultimately discover how to achieve it. It's important not to contemplate how in the beginning—it gets in the way and creates obstacles. If you're passionate about something, you'll figure it out.

> *"I began to look inside and answer some important questions about the kind of person I am. What are my gifts? What am I best at? Today, I know."*

K.H. / **Any resources or books you turned to?**

L.E. / Acupuncture books, of course. But mostly I made sure I was only around supportive people. I didn't want people asking questions like "Can you make a living doing that?" I wanted to move toward what I wanted to do and figure it out.

K.H. / **How do you measure your success?**

L.E. / It's pretty simple—I love to go to work. I never said that before. I love to go to my office. The money is a motivator, but it is not primary. That is one of the bonuses. I feel successful because I love what I am doing, and I think I make a difference in other people's lives.

GET FINANCIALLY FIT

Whatever your motivation, you still need to be pragmatic. For most people, a midcareer restart comes with a financial price tag, particularly if you don't have the cushion of a partner's income or a retirement or severance package. It might mean a sizable pay cut to pursue work in a more altruistic field, a hefty tuition bill for more schooling, or a temporary loss of medical and retirement benefits.

Before you plunge into a more rewarding second career, it pays to make a financial plan that will allow you to stick with your goals. If you're likely to trade a good income for better work, first review your entire financial life, from everyday expenses to retirement funding and health insurance costs. Then consider some of these money moves:

CHART A BUDGET. If you're going to be living on less, you probably need to trim expenses. Get a clear sense of your income, debts, and savings. If you don't already have a monthly savings system, start one. Track your spending and ask what luxuries you can do without: Restaurants? Dry cleaning? Vacations? It's smart to have a cushion of up to six months of living expenses set aside for transition costs or unexpected emergencies.

DOWNSIZE. Depending on the real estate market where you live, it might make sense to move to a smaller home or even relocate to a cheaper area. You might refinance your mortgage or sell your home and downsize.

GET OUT OF DEBT. If possible, pay off outstanding high-interest credit card debts, college loans, and auto loans. This can take some time, but starting a new venture with as clean a balance sheet as you can will make a difference.

BACK TO SCHOOL

LEARN BEFORE YOU QUIT. If possible, keep your current job while you add the education you need for your new pursuit. Many employers offer tax-free tuition assistance programs—up to $5,250, not counted as taxable income—and the contribution doesn't have to be tagged to a full-degree program. You may have to repay the funds, though, if you don't stay with the company for a certain number of years afterward.

SEEK FINANCIAL AID. You don't need to be college age to get a subsidized loan—there's no age limit, and you're eligible as a part-time student, too. The federal aid formulas don't take into account your home equity or retirement accounts, and since you are an adult, a certain amount of your savings is protected—usually from $20,000 to $60,000—depending on your age and marital status. To apply for aid, complete the Free Application for Federal Student Aid (FAFSA) form at www.fafsa.ed.gov.

While it might be tempting to borrow from your home equity, you're better off with a low-interest Stafford loan (www.staffordloan .com). If you meet a financial needs test, the government will pay the interest for as long as you're enrolled in school. The interest is currently a fixed rate of 6.8 percent, compared with about 8 percent for a home equity loan. Many private lenders also offer loans, though rates will be higher.

RESEARCH SCHOLARSHIPS AND GRANTS. These, too, are available for older students, usually offered by associations, colleges, religious groups, and foundations. Try sites such as FastWeb.com to find what's available.

TAKE ADVANTAGE OF EDUCATIONAL TAX BREAKS. Depending on your income, you might qualify for the lifetime learning credit, worth up to $2,000 each year. There's no limit to the number of years you can claim the credit. Your student-loan interest may even be tax deductible, depending on your income level. For details on annually adjusted income restrictions, see IRS publication 970, IRS.gov, or the tax benefits guide at NASFAA.org.

TEN TIPS FOR PLANNING A WINNING
SECOND CAREER

(from career coach Beverly Jones, ClearwaysConsulting.com)

1. IT'S NEVER TOO EARLY TO START THINKING ABOUT YOUR NEXT ACT.
The longer time frame you have to plan, the better. Start working at age
fifty on a career you might not get around to until age sixty. If you have
lots of time, you can try out some ideas and possibilities, role-play, and do
a little bit of those things to see if that is the direction you want to go.

2. UNDERSTAND WHAT IS BEHIND YOUR DESIRE TO MAKE A CHANGE.
Maybe you are starting to become disillusioned with your work.
You're bogged down. Perhaps you're no longer on the way up. You're
not getting promoted as quickly as you were. For some people, it
takes some kind of crisis to realize they want to make a change.

3. GET YOUR LIFE IN ORDER. Here's the thing—it may be a second act,
but it's still your life, and you just have one life. So if your life is in order,
your second act comes more easily. Get rid of clutter, or pay off your
debts. Consider where a few small changes might make a difference.

4. ASK YOURSELF: WHAT DO I HAVE TO DO IN ORDER TO GET RESULTS? If
your intent is not to slow down as you age, make physical activity a daily
routine. If your plans include the need to connect to more people, make
sure you're participating in the right online social networks or clubs. Identifying the immediate next step is an important part of your ultimate goal.

5. RETROFIT YOUR LIFE. When you are physically fit, you have more
energy and are mentally sharper to face the challenges ahead. Fitness

is a huge issue. You have to be in good shape to start a new career later in life—it takes an incredible amount of strength and energy.

6. BE PRACTICAL. If you'd like to go to graduate school, maybe start by taking a night course. You don't have to enroll in a full-course load. Take one class at a time and reevaluate at the end of the semester. Hold yourself accountable for what you can handle. You can add more classes as your direction and motivation become clear.

7. GET IN TOUCH WITH YOUR INNER SELF. A second career is often a spiritual quest. You want to make a contribution or be connected with your inner desires and goals. Consider reading some of Deepak Chopra's books on spirituality and mind-body medicine.

8. BE SUFFICIENTLY OPEN TO CHANGE IN LIFE. Don't underestimate what your transition will bring. Career changers can go into mourning. All of a sudden, they realize how they miss their old career, and they are not really open to replacing those things.

9. THINK THROUGH WHAT IT'S GOING TO TAKE TO MAKE A CAREER MOVE. What are the things that are important in your life? What things are actively giving you pleasure that you might have to give up? What things are easier to let go of?

10. LOOK AT YOUR WHOLE LIFE, NOT JUST YOUR JOB. If you are thinking about a career change, it may be because you are missing something in your life. But your career may not be your whole life. Some people want a job that allows them to pursue their true passion—and that's okay, too.

A KID AGAIN UNDER
THE BIG TOP

When Donald Covington was a kid, he and his younger brother, Duncan, spent their summer days putting on backyard circuses at their Baltimore home. The devilish duo performed daring feats on bicycles and such, recruiting neighborhood kids to join in the fun.

Then each year, in late November, the Shrine Circus, produced by the Polack Bros. Circus, would set up shop in an old armory for a week, featuring top acts from all over the world. Covington would tag along with his father, who volunteered as an usher. "I remember sitting in the bleachers and hearing the echoing sounds of the animals, the people, the band, and the smells of cotton candy and popcorn. For me, it was the most exciting event of the year," he recalls.

Some things cling to you. In 1995, after thirty years in the navy, Covington took mandatory retirement. And the navy captain, who once flew from the decks of carriers during the Vietnam War, ran away with the circus. The nonprofit, old-fashioned, one-ring Big Apple Circus, to be precise, where he is the company manager for the 170-member traveling troupe and staff.

Covington lives on the road for forty-five weeks a year, shuttling from Boston to Atlanta with stops in ten cities or more. His trailer-home partner is the circus wardrobe supervisor—his wife of thirty-eight years, Janice—whom he met when she was a navy nurse. They have three grown children.

Retiring at fifty, Covington could have worked for a defense contractor or flown for an airline. But the circus had never been far from his heart. Throughout his naval career, he attended circuses around the world and wrote reviews for *Circus Report*, a trade publication. So when he broached the idea of working for a circus, his family was supportive. "They knew the circus was important to me," Covington says, "and although no one shared my passion, they understood."

He talked to people he knew in the circus world, from Ringling Bros. to Big Apple. They gave him a feel for the pros and cons. And although he had no specific job in mind, he sent off his queries based on his military skill set—administration and management (he had commanded squadrons of 250 people or more), crisis management, the ability to react to unusual situations, and an understanding of a life of constant travel.

"When you think about it, the military and the circus are probably closer than most people think," Covington says. "It's a small group working very hard to achieve a goal. You have lots of specialists, and each is critical to what's going on. You also have the frustrations of life on the road and constantly adjusting to keep things going."

Big Apple's cofounders, Paul Binder and Michael Christensen, first hired him as a purchasing manager in charge of buying everything from feed for the horses to replacement tires for the trucks. And financially, with full retirement pay and benefits, he could afford to accept a job paying about half of his annual military salary. Climbing the ladder wasn't a concern, either. "The advantage to starting over in my situation was I had no pressing requirement to move up and become a director of something," Covington says. "I am very pleased to be a part of what goes on and do whatever I can to make things work, and that's a nice place to be."

On a stop at New York City's Lincoln Center, where the circus resides in mid-January, Covington's cramped office trailer sits adjacent to Big Apple's modest-size royal blue big top. Inside, there's a forty-two-foot sawdust ring, surrounded by 1,700 seats, all within fifty feet of the action, creating an intimate setting for this classical circus.

"I can hear the music of the band," Covington says, "and walk over to watch the kids as they come into the tent and get the first look at the rigging, the seats, and the ring. At that moment, they simply say, 'Wow!' For me, that's heaven."

In a flash, he's ten years old again—and the circus is in town.

—— Q & A ——
LOOKING BACK

K.H. / **What did the transition mean to you personally?**
D.C. / I looked forward to it. I was very fortunate in that I came from something that I enjoyed—the navy—and landed at something I also enjoy. Unlike people who take mandatory retirement and desperately need to find something to do, I went into a second career that has been as equally rewarding as the first. I look forward to going to work every day. I like the people I work with, and I feel that what I do is important and making a contribution.

K.H. / **Were you confident in what you were doing? Any second-guessing?**
D.C. / I knew it was the right thing. There will always be surprises, but my lifestyle has been that way for as long as I can remember. The navy certainly taught me that there are going to be unexpected changes. That wasn't a big problem for me.

K.H. / **Was there anything you would have done differently?**

D.C. / If anything, I might have started a little bit sooner. I waited a little bit longer than I should have to do the research and make contacts or to look at possibilities. I was lucky that I found sympathetic ears when I talked to the people in the circus industry. They were eager to talk to me and very open about what I was getting into and what the options might be.

"The advantage to starting over in my situation was I had no pressing requirement to move up and become a director of something. I am very pleased to be a part of what goes on and do whatever I can to make things work, and that's a nice place to be."

K.H. / **What are some of the unexpected rewards? Surprises?**

D.C. / I was concerned about our daughter, Anne, who was still in high school at the time, and how it would affect her. Now looking back on it—and I think she would agree with me—being on the road with the circus was a great place for her to grow up and go to school. She got a unique background, and it's helped her be the person she is today.

On a deeper level, I didn't realize how proud it would make me feel. I never get tired of the circus. It's such a unique experience—the skills of the artists and the technical aspects of putting on a Broadway-quality show in a tent. I am part of the group that takes care of the details to be sure that things happen correctly, and I feel deeply proud of the result. I see it every day when people come and watch the show.

K.H. / **What role did financial rewards play in your decision to make a transition?**

D.C. / I had a retirement setup, so the move was not necessarily for the money. On the other hand, though, it is nice to still have a job and be able to continue to do the things we want to do. It means my wife and I are able to keep our home in San Diego, in addition to the RV we travel in. It also helps with paying off our kids' tuition bills.

K.H. / **How did your preparation make your transition easier?**

D.C. / Again, I was fortunate—the circus is something I have been interested in and passionate about my entire life, even before I ever considered it a second career. So I contacted everyone I knew who could offer advice and insight. I learned that the circus business is very forgiving to new people who pay their dues. It is up to you to learn the business, but the people are very supportive.

And my family was 100 percent behind my decision. My wife, Jan, has been quite supportive. We couldn't have done it otherwise. She understood the sacrifice that she would make, since the circus is really my passion. She's a nurse. That's her profession. The circus is something she is doing so we can be together—and believe me, I really appreciate it!

K.H. / **What advice do you give to people who ask about making a career transition?**

D.C. / I tell them to make the effort to find something that fits them. It doesn't always have to be connected with good works or giving back to the community. Find something that makes sense for you, do it well, and do it 100 percent. If you can make that match, then every-thing else becomes worthwhile.

It's also important to start as soon as you can. If you know some-thing that you want to do, talk to as many people as you can and do whatever research is appropriate so that you'll feel comfortable when it is time to make the move.

K.H. / **Any resources you turned to that were helpful?**
D.C. / The navy has a transition program for those who are retiring. It was a great help to me and gave me perspective on the outside world, beyond the military. It covered financial planning, the psychol-ogy of how my transition would affect not only me but my family, too. It didn't give me the answers, but it helped give me the steps I needed to take.

K.H. / **How do you measure your success?**
D.C. / It's going to work every day and feeling good about what I am doing, enjoying what I do. I think that is most important for me. I feel like I am in the right place, and I am committed to what I am doing.

SECOND ACTS FOR RETIREES

CHECK FOR HELP WITH CAREER MOVES. In the private sector, many U.S. corporations, small and large, are beginning to provide career coaches and counseling on a limited basis to help employees who have retired or lost their jobs. Increasingly, firms will put you in contact with career centers operated by area colleges or local government agencies offering workshops on résumé writing, career counseling, job fairs, and retraining programs.

DO A BACKGROUND CHECK. This is your time to be inquisitive. Ask a lot of questions about the inner workings of an organization and what the work entails on a day-to-day basis. It's all about preparation. Knowing as much as you can is key to setting realistic expectations.

GET YOUR FAMILY ON BOARD. If you have a family or partner, it's imperative that everyone understands the new path you're embarking on and what it will entail. This might mean financial belt-tightening at first or increased travel. They don't have to own your dream, but their support will help you get off to a good start.

DON'T LET AGE GET IN YOUR WAY. When it comes to starting a new job, be forewarned: age discrimination is real. There's a perception that people over fifty or sixty will be just passing through as a transition into retirement. "Employers are loath to hire someone who they think will be out the door in a year or two," says Marc Freedman, founder and CEO of San Francisco–based Civic Ventures, a nonprofit organization whose programs and research focus on social careers for baby boomers. But remember: it is never too late to start a second career. "The issue is not age but personal health, energy level, and an entrepreneurial spirit," the Transition Network's Betsy Werley says. You need to be willing to prove that you still have what it takes.

FEEL POSITIVE ABOUT WHAT YOU HAVE TO OFFER. Workers over fifty tend to be self-starters, know how to get the job done, and don't need as much hand-holding as those with less experience. A great benefit to being older is that you have a good deal of experience. And whether you realize it or not, you have a network. You have a lot more resources to draw on than people in their twenties and thirties.

THE MILITARY AS A MODEL

The major employer in this country that really knows how to help its employees prepare for a second act is the military. The Department of Defense Operation Transition Web site, www.turbotap.org, for instance, features a transition bulletin board with job postings from companies that hire veterans and their spouses. On average, about ten thousand ads featuring thirty thousand jobs are posted each day.

Transition assistance programs help service members make the shift from soldier, sailor, airman, or marine to civilian. The programs, available at most installations, usually offer a two- or three-day class that covers the skills vital to finding a civilian job. In fact, the Defense Department finds its offering so necessary that it is mandatory for those preparing to exit the military or retire. Some of the areas covered in the classes are résumé writing, networking, interviewing, and job hunting.

Many classes offer help with face-to-face job interviewing techniques and even how to dress for that meeting. Some provide sessions with private-sector business representatives who answer questions about opportunities in the job market and the skills that are essential to finding the best jobs. They hammer home ways for service members to sell their military experience, such as learning how to translate military jargon or acronyms that job interviewers might not be familiar with and how that skill might fit into their organization.

Transition counselors can decode some of that insider military speak into plain language to help bridge the gap between the two worlds. Other critical benefits of the military's transition program include job counseling for a spouse, relocation assistance services, help switching health insurance or other medical and dental coverage, counseling on the effects of career change on individuals and their families, and, importantly, financial planning assistance. While the military has been at the forefront of second career services, many corporations are now offering free sessions with career counselors and job placement pros to employees who have been downsized, laid off, or given an early-retirement package.

GREAT JOB SITES FOR OLDER BOOMERS

CAREERBUILDER.COM

WORKFORCE50.COM

SENIORS4HIRE.ORG

RETIREDBRAINS.COM

AARP.ORG

ENCORE.ORG

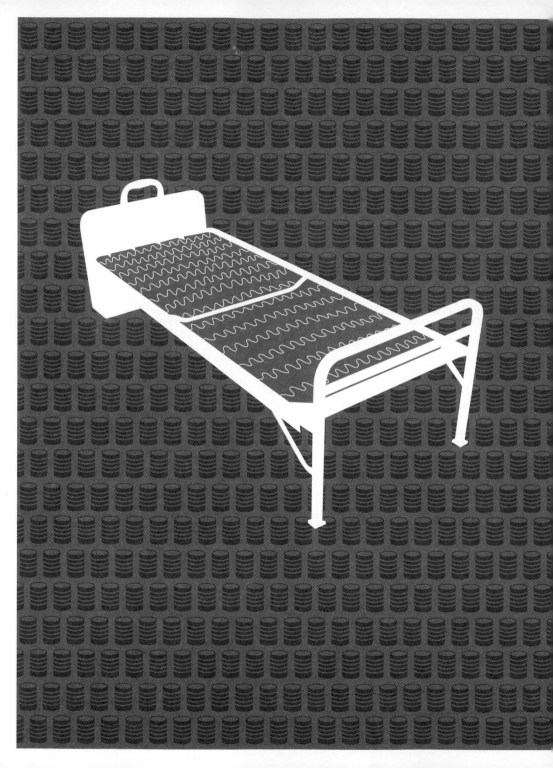

AT HOME WITH THE HOMELESS

When Anne Nolan first walked down the darkened steps into a homeless shelter, she started to cry. "I was so overwhelmed by the emotion of the place, the humanity, the pain," she recalls. "I was terrified and frightened. The dilapidated building was filthy, and it was mobbed with people lined up for food and shelter."

That was ten years ago. Today, Nolan, sixty-two, is president of Crossroads Rhode Island, the state's largest provider of care and shelter to the homeless. The nonprofit expects to serve some 7,500 people this year, from a newborn to an eighty-nine-year-old, and demand is growing. "When our consumer base grows, that's not a good thing," Nolan notes. "And we're busting at the seams."

Spoken like the veteran of corporate America that Nolan is. Her career path included stints as a university professor (she has a master's in counseling and a doctorate in education) and nearly thirty years working for big companies like Fleet Financial Group and Digital Equipment in various senior executive slots.

But by 1999 her everyday world was . . . flat. "There was no passion," Nolan says. Big salaries and year-end bonuses had kept Nolan tied to those corporate posts. "I got so far away from where my heart had been back in my idealist days growing up in the sixties.

I had started my career in education with such energy and enthusiasm and a belief that I could make a difference." At fifty-two, she was years from retirement. But when her company dissolved, she had the chance to step off the corporate merry-go-round, with a year's pay to tide her over.

She started to walk six or seven miles a day along the Blackstone River with her dog. "I wanted to do something that would make me proud, something to feel passionate about. Something that would make me cry for good reasons," she says. And one day, something shifted. "'That's it,' I said out loud. 'I'm not going back to the corporate world. I'm going to work for a not-for-profit.'" Nolan heard about Travelers Aid, the old name for Crossroads, arranged to meet with the president, and paid that first visit to a shelter. "I knew I had found my place," she says. Whenever Nolan bought a lottery ticket and dreamed of what she would do if she won, it was always the same fantasy: start a nonprofit to help homeless families. A strange choice, she says, considering that her only exposure to homeless people was stepping around them on city streets.

Impressed with Nolan's corporate background, the president named her to a board position that first day. Later, when the president left, Nolan got the job. The pay: only about half her six-figure corporate compensation. She did belt-tightening and tapped into her home equity—all worth it, she says. "I love my job. You can't put a price on that."

It turns out that her corporate career had readied her to help the homeless. "I held a patchwork of unrelated positions and industries that suddenly all connected. Whether it was financial controls or organizational development, environmental construction or an FDIC audit—suddenly it was all relevant."

Nolan used her business acumen to transform Crossroads Rhode Island into more than just a shelter and soup kitchen. Yes, food and shelter are available 24/7, but there is also a range of housing options, full-spectrum health care and dental service, basic adult literacy and GED training, and job search help. There's a nursing assistant training program, plus hands-on instruction in printing and graphics.

Crossroads has helped over thirty-three thousand adults and children over the past eight years. The nonprofit's annual budget is now about $11 million, up from some $3 million when Nolan started, as the number of donors has grown nearly tenfold. She says she has even bigger dreams for Crossroads. Nolan still cries sometimes when she enters the shelter, but it's no longer from despair.

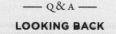

— Q & A —
LOOKING BACK

K.H. / **What did the transition mean to you personally?**

A.N. / I hate to sound corny, but I felt like a weight was lifted from me. My corporate career had lost its focus and meaning, and over the years, it just got heavier and heavier. I didn't even realize how much it had been weighing me down. I also gained an incredible sense of appreciation for my own life. I don't think a day has gone by that I haven't felt grateful for the little things. I think I lost that in my corporate career.

K.H. / **Were you confident in your decision to make this transition? Any second-guessing?**

A.N. / I never second-guessed my decision. And that was interesting because I got a lot of discouraging remarks. People told me I had no business thinking I could all of a sudden decide to work for a nonprofit, because I didn't have any experience. A nonprofit recruiter actually told me I should stay in corporate and just make donations! She was really rude. She basically said, "Who do you think you are? People have been working for thirty years in the nonprofit world and you just want to parachute in."

But I just knew. In this case, it was just so clear to me. I thought, no, you're wrong. I know where I belong.

"I wanted to do something that would make me proud, something to feel passionate about. Something that would make me cry for good reasons."

K.H. / **Was there anything you would have done differently?**
A.N. / I'm not sure there was anything I could have done differently.

K.H. / **How did your preparation help you succeed?**
A.N. / It is very cliché, but I followed what the books say. I got out there. I networked. I met as many people as I could. I did this spiderweb of contacts and networking. And I had volunteered beforehand.

Once I made the decision that I wanted to work for a nonprofit, and this one in particular, I joined the board. I was asked to, which was great. I just followed their rules of how to get the job.

There is no magic. All my skills from my corporate experience translated, and that was an important piece of the puzzle. It is very clear to me that the profit and nonprofit worlds are merging—as more and more things like compliance, regulations, and scrutiny are now applied to the nonprofit world. I was able to use the right language, and I think it has been to Crossroads' advantage that I have that corporate background.

And my skills were not the only thing I felt prepared me. I was also realistic about my weaknesses. There were things I knew nothing about, and I knew when to get help.

K.H. / **How big a role did potential financial rewards play in your decision?**

A.N. / None whatsoever. In fact, I remortgaged my house once again, and it has been worth every ounce of debt I incurred.

K.H. / **What are some of the unexpected rewards you have experienced?**

A.N. / I didn't expect it to be as much fun—but I have fun every day. We laugh hysterically here. I love the people I work with, both the clients and staff. I also didn't expect the diversity of the job. One minute I'm in Washington talking to senators, and the next minute I'm with a family in need. It is just amazing to me.

K.H. / **What do you tell others who come to you seeking advice about making a transition?**

A.N. / You have to know what you want to do. That's the hard part— really feeling right about your decision. I always tell people to take their time. When I was making my own decisions, I walked all the time with my dog. Everybody has a different way of processing. They have to find what that is and take the time to really understand their options and not do anything rash. I advise people to spend time with this kind of self-exploration, until they know.

K.H. / **Any resources you turned to?**

A.N. / Well, there is the old classic, *What Color Is Your Parachute?* I read it years and years ago.

K.H. / **How do you measure your success?**

A.N. / It's the fact that when Sunday night comes around, I have no dread. I look forward to Monday morning. And as long as I can look forward to Monday morning, I know I am doing the right thing.

The most important thing is making the decision and understanding what it is that you really want to do. For everybody, it's different. Mine just happens to be running a homeless program. For some people, it may be running a bookstore. I don't think the same answer applies to every question.

REASON TO VOLUNTEER

The Serve America Act, signed into law in 2009, features "Encore Fellowships"—one-year leadership and management positions specifically geared toward helping people over fifty-five transition to nonprofit or public sector careers. The fellowships will be available nationwide, with a maximum of ten per state, for individuals age fifty-five and older who work with nonprofits and government in areas of "national need," such as education, health, energy, the environment, and poverty.

The fellowships include a stipend of at least $22,000, with government funding of $11,000 at least matched by the sponsoring agency or organization. In addition, training, leadership development, and outplacement services are included in the program, which is modeled on a pilot encore fellowship program in California's Silicon Valley sponsored by Civic Ventures, publisher of Encore.org.

In addition to the new Encore Fellowships, the Serve America Act creates additional opportunities to use paid national service as a pathway to a public-service second career. At least 10 percent of the AmeriCorps positions created by the act are targeted at people over fifty-five. The total size of AmeriCorps is slated to grow from 75,000 currently to 250,000 by 2017, creating more than 25,000 positions a year for people who have finished their careers midlife and are looking for a second, or third, act.

WHERE TO FIND VOLUNTEER PROJECTS

There's no question that giving back feels good, but it can also offer a sense of whether a certain career field truly inspires you. Volunteering packs a threefold punch for career changers: it keeps existing professional skills up-to-date, bolsters your résumé, and, importantly, adds new contacts. A myriad of online services can connect you with both short-term and long-term volunteer projects that match your interests.

VOLUNTEER.GOV is a one-stop shop for public-service volunteer projects sponsored by the U.S. government.

USASERVICE.ORG, originally created to facilitate volunteering on National Service Day (held annually in January), lets unregistered visitors "find an event" (that is, a volunteer opportunity) and sign up to participate.

VOLUNTEERMATCH.ORG allows you to search more than fifty-four thousand listings nationwide. Its extensive database of projects lets you screen for everything from board opportunities to communications positions based on your interests and geographical location.

BOARDNETUSA.ORG places people on the boards of nonprofits. You fill out a profile of your interests and professional skills; nonprofits then choose whether to interview you for their board positions.

IDEALIST.ORG offers leads to more than fourteen thousand volunteer opportunities nationwide, plus internships and jobs in the nonprofit sector.

1-800-VOLUNTEER.ORG offers a database of volunteer projects nation-wide and allows you to search by county.

TAPROOTFOUNDATION.ORG places teams of highly skilled pro-fessionals who are doing pro bono consulting to help a local nonprofit increase its impact. Assignments are based on your pro-fessional experience. It operates in seven U.S. cities in a variety of fields, including finance, marketing, and information technology. Its volunteers work in teams of five (they can do so remotely) for at least five hours a week, for periods of five months.

ASHOKA.ORG supports the work of social entrepreneurs. Volunteers are needed to translate documents and assist with fundraising, marketing, Web site design, research, writing, graphic design, and technical support.

OPERATIONHOPE.ORG seeks volunteers with a background in the financial industry (mortgage brokers, bankers, tax consultants, etc.) to work as virtual volunteers, providing ongoing case management from any location with Internet access to victims of hurricanes and other disasters, offering financial and budget counseling over the phone. Volunteers receive training and software and can work from their home or office.

LAWYERSWITHOUTBORDERS.ORG directs legal pro bono services and resources to human rights initiatives, legal capacity-building proj-ects, and rule-of-law projects around the world. It seeks volunteers with a legal background—practicing or retired lawyers, law students, and others who have worked as legal support staff—to manage projects and sustain home and branch office operations. Volunteer tasks can include newsletter editing and layout, grant writing, graphic design, program development, and management.

RED CROSS VIRTUAL JOURNALISTS PROGRAM is an outlet for those with a background in journalism or communications to write articles for the Volunteer News section of RedCross.org.

ONLINEVOLUNTEERING.ORG is the United Nations database to find online volunteering opportunities with organizations that serve communities in developing countries.

DOCTORSWITHOUTBORDERS.ORG is an international medical humanitarian organization created by doctors and journalists in France in 1971. Today, Doctors Without Borders provides aid in nearly 60 countries to people whose survival is threatened by violence, neglect, or catastrophe, primarily due to armed conflict, epidemics, malnutrition, exclusion from health care, or natural disasters.

WHAT IS THE PEACE CORPS?

According to its Web site, the Peace Corps traces its roots and mission to 1960, when then senator John F. Kennedy challenged students at the University of Michigan to serve their country in the cause of peace by living and working in developing countries. From that inspiration grew an agency of the federal government devoted to world peace and friendship.

Since that time, more than 195,000 Peace Corps volunteers have served in 139 host countries to work on issues ranging from AIDS education to information technology and environmental preservation. They've been teachers and mentors to countless children. They've helped farmers grow crops, worked with small businesses to market products, and shown women how to care for their babies. More recently, they've helped schools develop computer skills and educated entire communities about the threat of HIV/AIDS. For more information, see www.peacecorps.gov.

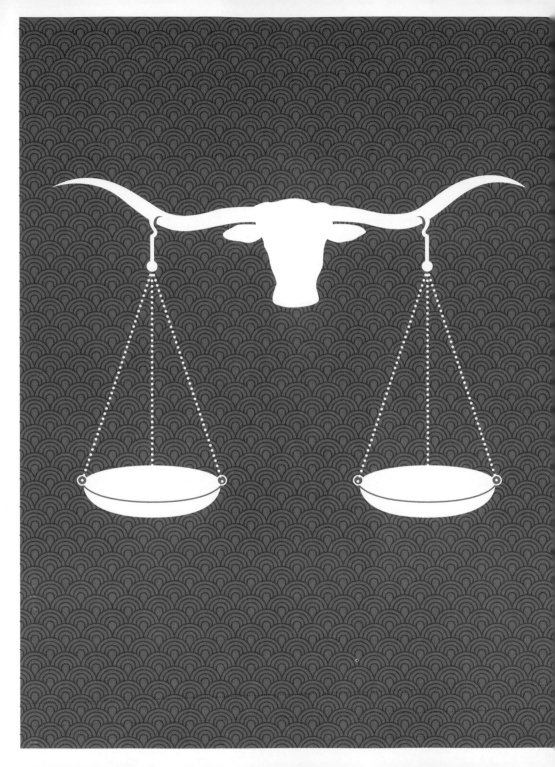

A LAWYER DOES BUSINESS WITH NEW PARTNERS

Sam Fox is not a gentleman farmer. But by all rights, the sixty-eight-year-old, once high-powered patent attorney could be.

Maybe even a city slicker to boot: Fox spent nearly his entire life in Washington, D.C., before retiring as managing partner from Sterne, Kessler, Goldstein & Fox, an intellectual-property law firm.

Today, Fox raises purebred polled Hereford cattle and harvests hay at his 187-acre spread outside Sperryville, Virginia, in the shadow of the Shenandoah Mountains. His crew of farmhands consists of his wife, Elizabeth, and a yellow Labrador retriever named Gus.

His hours are long—maybe even longer than those seven-day weeks he spent working in the firm's early days. Now he starts at first light and runs into the wee hours during calving season.

In 1988 Fox acquired the run-down, termite-infested stable and rolling land as an investment. He bought it the day he saw it. "Visually, it was just extraordinary," he says. Very quickly, he became "totally smitten with the countryside, the people, and the way of life. Pretty soon, I was looking for something that would allow me to be here and have something to do as well."

He succeeded. It began with a rebuilding of the courtyard-style stable, square foot by square foot, into a home. It evolved into a farming business in 1998, when he purchased four pregnant cows from a neighbor. "I had been spending a lot of money on this place, doing everything from the building to the fencing, and I thought there could be a way to turn this into a business," he says.

Knowing that Fox was in the country only on weekends, the same neighbor volunteered to keep the cows for him. He also became Fox's mentor on the ways of cattle farming and haymaking. Other neighbors have pitched in, too, to help him find his way in the country. "They know I am trying," he says, "and they don't think less of me because I don't know something."

Fox started by visiting the property every Sunday. Progress was slow. First, electricity was added, and next, a well was drilled for running water. Then he logged the one-hour, forty-minute trip from Washington for the entire weekend. Before he knew it, he was devoting every spare minute to the farm. "Instead of taking vacations at the beach, I came here," he says. In time, Fox realized that he wanted to be able to work on the farm and do it full time while he was still relatively young.

The learning curve has been steep. "I lost a calf the other day because I didn't realize the heifer was in trouble. Next time, I'll know," he says.

And the carpentry needed to make the place livable was far more than he had imagined. "If I had known the extent of the work the place needed, I never would have undertaken it," he says. "I wasn't born for this. I didn't work in the building trades. As I made my way around the building, stud by stud, I thought, at any minute, this whole thing is going to come down."

But the intrinsic rewards are many for this city boy: "I feel like I have built something really beautiful, and that's very satisfying to me. I'm proud of it." For Fox, it's proof that "you can make anything happen as long as you are willing to work at it."

He now owns thirty-two cows, five heifers, one steer, and two bulls. This spring, thirty calves were born, most of which will be sold at auction. About half of the land is in pasture or hay production, the balance wooded.

While the farming business is not generating profits, the operation doesn't need to do so. The Foxes' retirement savings are enough to cover their living expenses. But this year, if the auction prices hold up, Fox hopes his operation will break even. That is tough when costs keep rising from fertilizer to grain and cattle prices are down. One of the problems affecting the industry, Fox explains, is that dairy prices have dropped, and many dairy farmers are getting out of the business. "I read that in Wisconsin alone they are going to cull four hundred thousand animals out of the dairy herd, and all that goes into the meat market."

Fox is toying with trying to develop a market where he could sell directly to the consumer, and he could raise his cattle entirely on grass and organically. For now, though, it remains a calf/cow operation, which sells off the calves to a middleman long before they're sold for meat. Fox revels in the challenging process of breeding quality cows and raising young calves—even those that require bottle-feeding by hand, as two who lost their mothers did this past spring.

"I never loved being a lawyer," Fox says. "I enjoyed managing the firm and loved the people there. But the farm is my real passion." He doesn't actually see himself as the owner, but rather, the steward of the property—looking after it for the next people who come through.

LOOKING BACK

K.H. / **What did the transition to a second career mean to you personally?**

S.F. / I reacted so emotionally to this land, this terrain. I was really looking forward to being here. I wanted to live here. I never loved practicing law. I wanted a different life, living in the country, working outside—I can honestly say I had very few regrets about leaving the law firm. I miss the people, but I didn't miss the type of stress that I had. I feel bound to this place. I have a greater feeling and sense of responsibility for the animals than I'd ever thought I would.

K.H. / **Any second-guessing?**

S.F. / Never did.

K.H. / **Anything you would have done differently?**

S.F. / I would have done it thirty years earlier!

K.H. / **How did your preparation help you?**

S.F. / I was able to gradually prepare myself and get involved little by little. The first ten years I was here, I just worked on the building itself. During that time, I enrolled in a range of classes on farming. While I was still a lawyer, I took courses in cow/calf management at the University of Virginia, for example. They offered class work on various topics, including health, birthing issues, and things of that nature. It taught me the real nuts and bolts of how to run a successful operation from a business as well as an agricultural and veterinary perspective.

My previous life experience played a big role, too. Before practicing law, I had a business in the chemical industry, and I learned to do electrical and plumbing work. I have always been interested in woodworking and had basic carpentry skills. I was also interested in mechanics, which helped when it came to maintaining all the farm equipment. Because of those previous interests, I was better prepared to come out and live and work on the land.

Ultimately, I was never afraid to ask questions. I have no pride about that. I continue to learn all the time.

K.H. / **How do you measure your success?**

S.F. / There are many levels to it: How am I caring for the land? Am I doing a good job? Have I improved the immediate environment? Am I treating my cattle appropriately?

When I practiced law, I had lots of anxious moments, and they all revolved around money. Now I am dealing with the lives of animals. It is a completely different level of responsibility. There are nights when I can't sleep because a calf's just been born, and it's cold out. Is it all right? Should I go out at midnight? At 2 A.M.?

There's still a lot of anxiety for me, but seeing a healthy calf at its mother's side is the greatest reward.

K.H. / **What do you tell others who ask your advice about starting a new career?**

S.F. / Most people think I'm crazy! Rarely does anyone ask me for advice. But if they did, I'd tell them that retiring is not an easy thing to do. I know people who flunked retirement. They don't know what to do with themselves.

What was different for me was that I had a true passion about what I wanted to do. I felt directed toward this life. I even tried to figure out how to retire by the end of 2000. There was something significant about making the transition at the end of the century. I did stay on part-time for a couple more years, so I didn't leave the firm high and dry.

The other thing that made it possible was that my life partner was fully supportive. Elizabeth never ever said, "Hey, this is a bad idea," or

"Are you sure you want to do this?" She knew it was what I wanted to do, and she has always loved it out here, too.

Elizabeth is fully involved in the farming operation. She is very intuitive. Having her help and support has been key to making this change. There are plenty of times when I don't know what I'm doing, and we'll talk it over—having Elizabeth with me makes a huge difference.

"I feel like I have built something really beautiful, and that's very satisfying to me. I'm proud of it. You can make anything happen as long as you are willing to work at it."

K.H. / **Any books or resources you found helpful?**
S.F. / *The Merck Veterinary Manual.*

K.H. / **What were some of the unexpected rewards? Surprises?**
S.F. / I have always felt a little bit like an outsider no matter what I've done. I started practicing law later in life, and I never really felt like a lawyer. I moved to the farm and never exactly felt I was a farmer. And there are certain people here who resent outsiders. But there are people who've made me feel appreciated because they realized what my level of commitment was. They could see that. And I've been pleasantly surprised by the acceptance that I have received from certain portions of the community.

I realize now that I am a farmer. That's what I do. I'm not a lawyer out here fiddling around. I'm not a lawyer at all anymore.

We're farming. That's what we're doing. There's no way to make any money, but it's the grandest life you could ever hope for. I'm not a city boy anymore. I don't think of myself as someone who comes here on weekends. This is my home. This is all there is for me.

SLOW AND STEADY

TALK TO PEOPLE. Find people who are currently doing the work you want to be doing, and seek their advice and counsel. Finding a real pro who is willing to show you the ropes can make the transition into a new field a much easier journey. They have valuable expertise you can learn from. Take the time to nurture these relationships. You may find them in unlikely places—from the local hardware store to a conference—so be open to a variety of sources.

UPGRADE YOUR SKILLS AND EDUCATION. Chances are you'll need to bone up on new skills and maybe even earn another degree. If possible, take required courses before you quit your current job. Professional programs, grad schools, and community colleges offer evening and weekend classes that you can fit into your existing schedule without having to make a major move. Your current employer might even foot the bill, but make sure you check the fine print—you might have to repay tuition expenses if you leave your job within a certain time frame.

START SMALL AND GIVE YOURSELF TIME TO GROW AND LEARN. If possible, start your new venture with baby steps and let it evolve. Making a change in stages allows you to work at something you are passionate about without taking a wild leap. In time, you may be able to grow a hobby into a profitable enterprise.

DON'T BE AFRAID TO ASK QUESTIONS. Bury your pride or fear of sounding stupid or naive. It never hurts to ask others for help.

Being a newcomer is always uncomfortable, particularly if you were in a position of authority in your old line of work. If you want to learn, you have to be willing to set all that aside and simply admit you don't know something. You're sure to find plenty of others who have asked those same questions along the way and will be more than happy to pass on the favor.

BOTTLING A HEALTHY IDEA

Running—and finishing—a 5K race wasn't always on Trish May's to-do list. But on a crisp June day in 1994, May, now fifty-six, completed her first race. She joined hundreds of breast cancer survivors along Seattle's Lake Washington on the annual Shore Run to benefit research. Nearing the finish line, surrounded by cheering supporters, she was exhausted and in tears. "I remember thinking to myself, if I can finish this race, I can beat cancer," she says.

The experience motivated her to help fight the disease. It would, however, be five more years until May resigned as director of marketing and strategic planning at Microsoft and began to assemble her dream company, Athena Partners. It's a nonprofit corporation that sells Athena bottled water and donates 100 percent of the net proceeds to women's cancer research. "My mission is to raise funds and awareness to help make real research progress," May says.

She also needed time for her battle with breast cancer, diagnosed in 1993, and to deal with her mother's death from ovarian cancer that same year. May underwent six months of chemotherapy, six weeks of radiation, and five years on the anti-estrogen drug tamoxifen—as well as surgeries for additional lumps.

Initially, her diagnosis prompted her to get involved with cancer fundraising. But she staked out the larger goal of using her business skills to raise money to find a cure.

May had landed at Microsoft in 1985 at the age of thirty-one with an MBA and four years of marketing experience with Golden Grain Macaroni Company. She rose through a series of marketing positions and was a prime mover behind the product that became Microsoft's PowerPoint. By 1999, savings from her six-figure salary and the stock options packaged with it easily enabled her to retire comfortably.

May could have opted for a lifestyle of private jets, worldwide travel, and charity boards, but instead she chose to work. So did her husband, Peter, a University of Washington political science professor. May did, however, exchange seventy-hour work weeks for a mere forty to fifty hours a week—but no salary.

"I knew I could write a check for a million dollars, but it wouldn't necessarily go very far. I needed to invest some money and let it grow and generate an annuity that over time would continue to contribute," she says. And that's where her marketing prowess took over.

In the summer of 2002, May sat on the floor of her home in the Seattle suburbs, with three large grocery bags of mostly natural or organic goods spilled around her. She combed through yogurts and energy bars, looking for a product around which to build a company that would generate cash for research on breast and gynecological cancer.

As she sipped from a bottle of water, it hit her—water. It is healthy, ubiquitous, and inexpensive. By choosing a commodity, she could create a brand where the cause would be the star. The brand name would be Athena, the Greek goddess of wisdom and war.

May sank over $500,000 in personal funds into her start-up and introduced Athena bottled water to consumers in July 2003. The water is purified tap water with added minerals, similar to Dasani. Using Paul Newman's charitable food company, Newman's Own, as a model for outsourcing production, distribution, and transportation, May concentrated on marketing and building partnerships.

Athena is now the official bottled water on Alaska Airlines and at Seattle's Qwest Center and is currently available at five thousand outlets in seven western states. A giant food-distribution company, Sysco—which stocks corporate cafeterias, delis, and coffee shops—currently distributes the bottled water, and plans call for it to be available nationwide. The result: this year Athena is expected to sell sixteen million bottles (up from ten million four years ago) and deliver revenues of $2.5 million. The company also launched a brand extension, Athena premium dark chocolates, in October 2008. In one quarter, the firm sold $1 million of chocolate.

Even for a nonprofit with just two salaried employees, bottom-line proceeds in the extremely competitive bottled water category are slim, but they can add up. To date, Athena has contributed $200,000 to organizations, including the Fred Hutchinson Cancer Research Center, the Marsha Rivkin Center for Ovarian Cancer Research, and the University of Washington's UW Medicine.

"At Microsoft, you had to be the champion of your own product and find creative ways to extend your reach," recalls May. "We were in a hurry."

Sounds familiar.

— Q & A —
LOOKING BACK

K.H. / **What did the transition mean to you personally?**

T.M. / I had cancer in 1993, and I had been holding my breath every year, hoping that I was going to live to the next year. We launched our product in 2003, which was the ten-year mark. It was a turning point for me, partly because my mother had passed away ten years after her first diagnosis of cancer. I was also forty-nine years old at the time and thinking about the next decade. I was ready to move on. My cancer was the catalyst, but all those factors converged to make me ready, willing, and able to do this.

Then the willing and able part: my background and working at Microsoft gave me the resources, the skill, and a little bit of courage, a little chutzpah. That confidence in my own abilities gave me the passion and the drive to make something happen.

The third piece was the nonprofit side. I had, as a result of the other two, started to explore the nonprofit arena. By the time I was ready to launch the business, I had about five years of being out in the community working with other nonprofits, interacting with other people who had started nonprofits, and starting to get that perspective and that experience.

The fourth, I would say, was the supportive climate in general of a group of people, especially in Seattle, who wanted to start new ventures whether they were nonprofits or for-profits, whether it was venture capital or social enterprises. Seattle was this microcosm of a lot of activity—still is—but especially at that point. So personally all those things were coming together to really give me the passion and the drive and put me forward on this new trajectory.

K.H. / **Any second-guessing along the way?**
T.M. / Yes and no. I was confident, and I felt good about the direction I had chosen.

I, by nature, am somebody who wants to take risks, and I was seeking a change, so that was all part of the experience. Having cancer really changed my outlook on what every day meant—the challenges of cancer puts everything else into perspective, so things don't seem as hard. Every day is unexpected and that is kind of the beauty of it.

So I did some second-guessing along the way, but to me it was helpful.

I made some key strategic decisions early on about how we would run the organization, but I was continually making refinements and adjustments.

The first was that we would be self-funding and not seek outside venture capital money. That inherently limited our scale. I also felt my expertise was tied to consultative marketing, and so we built a Web site of cancer resources using content from others, not by creating new material. Finally, we wanted to find our own niche and add value in a special way—instead of the classic nonprofit approach of events and fundraisers, we would derive our income by selling products.

Periodically I would go back and think, were those the right things to do? But overall, I came back to those several key premises and I kept true to them. They fit my personal goals and financial capabilities.

K.H. / **What were some of the unexpected rewards? Surprises?**

T.M. / There were two. One was the hugely positive consumer response. I anticipated that we would have a novel approach, but what I didn't anticipate (and what has become the fuel that drives me every day) is the way in which the community has embraced Athena—and the fact that we can operate with two people on staff.

We tapped into an idea that something as simple as a bottle of water can make someone feel empowered to make a difference—it makes them feel part of something larger. They are giving back and spreading the word about the cause. And that has been incredibly rewarding and positive for me. Every day, I get an inspiring piece of feedback, whether it is a phone call or a letter.

The other surprise is that it's been like building or remodeling a house—it's a lot harder than I'd expected. There are so many things that came along that I didn't anticipate, and it's been expensive and challenging. When we first got started, I didn't quite appreciate how much time, effort, and money it would take to launch this new organization and product.

We chose a very self-sufficient model, but perhaps it would have been better to grow a bit larger. Newman's Own has always been our model and my inspiration, but the smaller scale is challenging. I also work fifty to sixty hours a week now. It's less than I worked at Microsoft—but at Microsoft, I could take a real vacation. I have not taken a nonworking vacation in six years!

"There is nothing more fulfilling than to be part of something larger than yourself."

K.H. / **How big a role did financial rewards play in your decision to make the transition?**
T.M. / I wanted to help others become empowered, to be part of this. There was no financial reward for me. In fact, it was the exact opposite. It was completely a personal reward.

K.H. / **How did your preparation help you make the transition a success?**
T.M. / I had retired in 1999, so I had a year or two to refresh and regroup. I went out and investigated ideas for our product and relied on my marketing contacts and the Internet to learn about the water business. I didn't have the resources I was used to at Microsoft. It was all about pulling myself up by my bootstraps to find ideas.

I cold-called the chief operating officer at Newman's Own. That was a pivotal experience for me. I didn't expect that they would meet with me, but I thought, "What the heck! I'll call them up." And the COO sat down with me for two hours. He was very generous with his time. They were a $250 million business running with fourteen people. That really laid the groundwork for me in terms of my approach. The perspective, the wisdom, and the guidance that he gave me were very beneficial.

Ultimately, it came down to the fact that I did a lot of research. I spent about six months to a year preparing myself—learning about the nonprofit side, the profit side, the water and packaged goods side—and then I had to make the leap.

K.H. / What do you tell others who come to you seeking advice about making a career change?

T.M. / Be prepared for the challenge and also be prepared for the unexpected rewards. It is a marathon, not a sprint. There's a lot of excitement at first, but it quickly moves into how to make things run day to day.

So follow your dream and passion, absolutely! Do it, if you can, because it is so rewarding. That sounds trite, but I don't know how else to put it. Every day I wake up and think about what choices I have. I have chosen to take my life to another level. It's a different realm, a different path. There is nothing more fulfilling than to be part of something larger than yourself.

K.H. / How do you measure your success?

T.M. / In the short term, it's about people championing the cause and empowering others. It's the awareness we are creating.

In the long term, I hope it generates more money. We have been cash-flow positive, which is pretty remarkable for a small business—especially in the beverage industry, going head to head with Coke and Pepsi every day. And we've done it on a shoestring. I ultimately believe we are building a brand that will contribute significant funds to women's cancer research.

But perhaps the best measure of success is the satisfaction of waking up every morning and choosing this life, choosing Athena.

K.H. / **Were there any books or resources you found helpful?**
T.M. / I read a number of books and stories from other people who started socially responsible businesses, such as Ben Cohen's *Ben & Jerry's Double-Dip: How to Run a Values-Led Business and Make Money, Too*.

But the best resources were colleagues and networking. A lot of it was uncharted territory because our approach was a hybrid of using traditional business principles to advance a social cause. Part of the fun was cobbling together my own set of resources and charting a course that others hadn't already identified.

THINKING OF STARTING A NONPROFIT ORGANIZATION?

Starting a nonprofit is an exceptionally complicated process, but the payoff can be truly rewarding. One of the leading resources to help you get going is Idealist.org. This Web site offers in-depth guidance, lays out first steps for launching a new organization, and provides resources. According to the site experts, generally speaking, you will know you have a solid case for starting a new nonprofit if:

· You have a clientele or beneficiary with a bona fide need that's not being met by an existing nonprofit or program.

· You have an innovative programming idea or approach to meeting the need.

· You already have (or know how you can secure) the monetary and in-kind donations needed to support the organization for the foreseeable future.

—— EXPERT ADVICE ——
BEVERLY JONES, CAREER COACH

Beverly Jones offers advice with the unique position of one who's been there. In 1999, after more than two decades as a high-powered corporate lawyer, she took a golden parachute retirement package from her position as vice president of external affairs and policy at Consolidated Natural Gas. She was fifty-three.

At that age, Jones's working days were far from over. But she was ready for a break. In fact, she was eager for the respite after spending twenty-two years in a fast-paced legal career and paying her own way through a journalism degree and an MBA from Ohio University, followed by a Georgetown University law degree. "I desperately needed to recharge and map out my future," Jones says. "I had taken maybe two three-week vacations in my life. I knew now was the time to pause."

The prospect of going back to a full-time employer was daunting. "All I could think was that I'm no longer young and cute. All of a sudden I'm fifty-three and retired. I'm old. I was worried people wouldn't hire me at that age," she recalls.

When the scary notion of going to a Washington cocktail party without a good answer to the ubiquitous question, "What do you do?" arose, Jones quickly had a business card made up to hand out. It simply read: counselor, consultant, coach. "I didn't know that coaching was an established career, but it sounded good."

She passed the cards out that night, and the phone started ringing. "People wanted me!" she remembers with a laugh. Soon, people who had worked for her over the years began lining up at her door. "I had clients before I even knew what coaching was."

But it wasn't that surprising. It was the kind of attorney and boss she was. Jones's philosophy of managing had always involved trying to help people figure out their goals and ways to get there.

Jones had finally found her passion—mentoring others—even though she'd been practicing that her entire career. This time she took it on full time and launched her own coaching/consulting practice: Clearways Consulting. "Retiring with a modest pension gave me a little flexibility," she says.

Initially, she remained loosely associated with a law firm and did a little lobbying for a nonprofit. She began to study and obtained a Leadership Coaching Certificate from Georgetown University. She attended workshops, hired her own career coach, and read extensively about the field and related areas such as self-help, spirituality, and fitness. "In time, I began to find my own voice as a coach and felt confident I was doing what I was meant to do," Jones says.

Among her current clients today are attorneys, lobbyists, business owners, and executives. "Many are accomplished professionals, boomers nearing retirement—they all want to bring a new direction to their careers," says Jones.

Her own experience of switching jobs at midlife gives her the chops to back up what she preaches. "After building my own business for a decade, I know that age is not a limitation or a barrier."

ARE YOU READY FOR THE
NONPROFIT WORLD?

The answer may be yes, if:

- You have spent ample time understanding the world of non-profits, being out in the community working with other nonprofits, and interacting with other people who started nonprofits to glean their perspective and experience.

- You have completed the IRS paperwork for establishing a nonprofit entity. IRS publication 557 contains information on all the organizational categories and instructions on qualifying for and applying for 501(c) status.

- Funding to launch your company and sustain it for an adequate period is in place.

- You have scrupulously researched the industry and field you are entering and have a solid plan of action.

THE PERSONAL COST OF NONPROFITS, FROM IDEALIST.ORG

Even if you have a handle on the logistics of starting a nonprofit, be sure to consider the personal costs of doing this kind of work before you begin. Here are some of the realities for which nonprofit founders should be prepared:

The risk of burnout—from long hours, low or no pay, and the ultimate responsibility for the organization's success—is very real. It may be years before your organization's work is recognized, if it ever is. Many excellent organizations haven't received much or any acknowledgment for the good work they do.

Because the founder of a nonprofit is often the "face" of the organization, you must be comfortable with that kind of visible, public role. Especially at the outset, you will need the support of everyone you know.

You will need to be comfortable asking friends, relatives, community members, and anyone else in your network for support.

The decision to start a nonprofit should take into account the organization's short-term commitments as well as its long-term sustainability. The demands on a nonprofit founder are both constant and ever changing. Founders must recognize when it is time to step away and leave the leadership of the organization to a new generation. With all of the time, energy, and passion that go into starting and sustaining a nonprofit, separating your identity from that of your organization can be a true challenge.

BEVERLY'S GUIDE TO FINDING YOUR PASSION

FIND A PLACE TO START. You don't need a precise definition before you get going. Start by making a list of what you do know you want in the next phase of your career. If you are preoccupied with what you don't want, make a list and restate them in positive terms. For example, if you are determined to stop working sixty hours a week, you might add "forty-hour work week" to your wish list.

TAKE STEPS. Don't struggle to find an ideal starting point or perfect path. Once you have some picture of where you want to go, get things moving by taking small steps toward that vision. Your activity won't be linear and you don't need to plan out your steps in advance. What really matters is that you do a little something on a regular basis. Even if you just take one tiny step each week, at the end of a year you will have made some real progress toward change.

DON'T RUIN YOUR HOBBY. I love to garden. When I was thinking about what to do next I thought about being a landscape designer. But I quickly realized that I'd get lonely in the garden all day—I much prefer working with people. Gardening is a great hobby and escape from work, but it wouldn't be the right career move for me. Make sure you think hard about how your passion will become a new career.

STOP YOUR INNER ENEMY. If you have a negative refrain that goes through your head and sabotages your efforts to make a change—"I'm too old to do that"—make note of it. Write that thought down in a notebook and reframe it with a positive thought, such as, "I have these specific skills, and I'm going to use them in a new career." You need to get rid of that old blocking message to move forward with your dreams.

ASK THE BASIC QUESTIONS. Does your second act fit your lifestyle? Can you afford it? What does your partner think? Ask yourself how a certain career will work with your social patterns, your spending habits, and your family situation. It will help you to dig deeper and get a clearer picture of what you truly want in your life and your options to get there.

START A JOURNAL. Journaling is a great way to map your new career direction. Make lists: the best times in your life, the things you really like, the experiences you've enjoyed, what you've excelled at, the best moments in your current career. These lists will help you hone in on your passion and visualize yourself harnessing it to pursue something new and exciting.

GET A BUSINESS CARD. Want to be an artist but still working as a lawyer? Get an artist's card. As soon as you have a card, it makes the career real. You can get your second-act card long before you finish your first act. I immediately got cards that said counselor, consultant, and coach—simply because I couldn't bear the thought of going to a party without a business card. I passed them out, and by the end of the evening, I was a coach. Printing your new information on a card can be transformative.

BARKING UP THE RIGHT TREE

As a kid, Deborah Langsam used to stare in the windows of the bakeries in Brooklyn, New York, and dream of what delicacy she would buy if she had all the money in the world.

As co-owner of Barking Dog Chocolatiers, an artisanal chocolate company in Charlotte, North Carolina, Langsam, a former associate professor of biology, no longer has to fantasize about indulging her sweet tooth. With her husband, Joel Fischer, a retired developmental pediatrician, she stirs up vats of silky chocolate and handcrafts it into mouth-watering truffles, barks, ganaches, and pastries in a state-of-the-art home kitchen.

Langsam, a botanist, retired after twenty-two years at the University of North Carolina at Charlotte. Fischer officially shuttered his medical practice fifteen years ago to focus on SupportWorks, a nonprofit clearinghouse he founded to help people find and form support groups and research medical information.

Before retiring from science and medicine, the couple took a six-week pastry course at the École Ritz Escoffier in Paris, alongside professional chefs. It was in the basement of the tony Ritz hotel that they fell madly in love with the process of making chocolate.

Not surprisingly, it was the science that intrigued them—the methodical experiments and technical precision needed to ensure a ganache that was smooth, not grainy.

Eventually, they journeyed around the United States, Canada, and beyond to train with expert pastry chefs and chocolatiers, honing the techniques of framing, molding, and panning. Finally, they began designing their own chocolates.

Their tempting morsels were a resounding success with friends, who pushed the couple to make chocolates to sell. In 2000 they officially started Barking Dog Chocolatiers, naming it in honor of a favorite pooch that barked only when she was hungry.

Annual candy sales fluctuate each year, but the sweet news is that all profits (neither Langsam nor Fischer earns a salary from Barking Dog) go to meet SupportWorks's annual budget, as well as other local charities that assist people with food or medicine.

It's a small business, and the couple aims to keep it that way. The chocolate making is still a two-person operation. In spurts, they might spend fifteen hours a day swirling up their elegant chocolates to fill customer orders from their Web site—sampler boxes, wedding novelties, or special orders with custom logos. And their candies and pastries are served as dessert at the Bonterra Dining & Wine Room, a Charlotte restaurant.

Their latest confection: The St. Bernard Collection, decadent milk chocolate truffles. The new candies sell for $20 for a box of ten truffles, but they can also be purchased at a $5 discount, "a mitzvah price" for those ordering for anyone with a very serious illness.

"For someone who is going through chemotherapy, for instance, or someone who is having trouble chewing, the truffles are easy to eat because they melt in your mouth," Langsam explains. "We created them for a dear friend who was battling cancer. The feedback has been amazing. And that's exactly why we do what we do."

There's plenty of downtime for Langsam to spend on her fabric art business, called Barking Dog Fiber Arts, which has taken off with juried and solo art gallery shows. All profits from those sales also go to charity. Plus, there's allotted time for Fischer to tend to SupportWorks, as well as for the duo to travel and take more chocolate courses. "We don't measure our self-worth by how much money comes in," Fischer says. "We don't want to get caught up in the American way of always getting bigger and bigger."

Langsam's decision to retire from academia stemmed in large part from "the constant pressure to do more," she says. "There was always another paper to write, a bigger grant to be awarded."

Deciding to leave her faculty post, even with full retirement benefits, wasn't easy. "I liked what I did very much," she says. "My identity was as a professor." Yet an early health scare with cancer, when she was in her thirties, had taught Langsam how short life can be. Was it really worth working so hard to be named a full professor? "It was an ego thing for me," Langsam says.

Sensible spending suits the couple's sweet new lifestyle—and they had always made do on modest salaries. They both drive fourteen-year-old Volvos and don't splurge on designer clothes or fancy jewelry.

"There is no way we could have planned this adventure," Fischer says. "It started out as a kick—something fun to do together. Now all we have to say is that we make chocolate and everyone smiles!"

—— Q & A ——

LOOKING BACK

K.H. / **What did the transition mean to you personally?**

D.L. / At first it scared me because it meant I was giving up my identity as a professor. But the career change has allowed me to enjoy my work and the process of creating something. Every once in a while I'll be on a deadline, and it reminds me of how much my life was once controlled by deadlines. It reminds me of how much I get pleasure from what I am doing now.

J.F. / Now we have second acts where we are able to work hard when we want—and then take a break. A couple years ago, we worked eighteen hours a day, six or seven days a week, getting the candy out. It keeps us really busy, but for relatively short periods of time, and then we're done. We love it.

K.H. / **Were you confident in what you were doing? Any second-guessing?**
D.L. / Once I left the university, there was no second-guessing. I have never regretted it for a minute. I've missed certain things. One of the things I really loved about my university work was teaching. But now Joel and I do chocolate tasting and teach chocolate-making techniques in small groups, so I get to do some of that in other ways.

K.H. / **Is there anything you would have done differently?**
J.F. / No. Well, there's always . . . wouldn't it have been nice to have started this a year earlier?

K.H. / **Any unexpected rewards or surprises?**
D.L. / There have been so many. I had no idea that things were going to open up for me as an artist. I had no idea that I would be doing shows or that one of my pieces would be used as a publicity shot for a gallery show. The biggest joy has been seeing doors open that we hadn't planned, seeing doors appear that we never thought about. Like having an article about us in *U.S. News & World Report*!

J.F. / This whole adventure has been a surprise.

K.H. / **What role did financial rewards play in your decision to make a move?**

D.L. / None—in the sense that we didn't need to make money to live on, so it wasn't as stressful. Even though we took a financial hit in our retirement accounts, we still feel we have enough saved to meet our needs. We live responsibly. We are able to say no to things that don't work for us and say yes to things that would be a good adventure. As a child of Depression-era parents, I had to get over my fear that we didn't have enough saved before I left the university job. But we're doing fine. It's all about giving back.

J.F. / Money is important in many ways, but it's not always the answer. For example, Costco contacted us about selling our chocolate, but we felt it would create too much stress and work. So we said no.

K.H. / **How did you prepare for the change?**

J.F. / I stepped out of my practice in stages and was able to gradually learn about cooking and making chocolate. We traveled and studied chocolate making by taking classes from masters. That was a no-brainer. Why not learn from people who have been doing this for thirty or forty years? It was obvious that we needed to do some kind of training, and the training was fun. Through various connections, I was able to volunteer at Dean & Deluca, making chocolate. I happened to be there on the day they needed an extra hand, and I just stayed on.

We overplanned things financially so we could afford to make the change. The planning allowed this to be an adventure that could take on a life of its own. We're able to make chocolate for people who are sick—that's fantastic.

D.L. / I want to add that we started small. At the very beginning we made chocolate for friends and relatives. Then we sold it at the restaurant here in Charlotte. Then we thought about starting a Web site. It has all evolved in its own time.

"The planning allowed this to be an adventure that could take on a life of its own. We're able to make chocolate for people who are sick—that's fantastic. Whatever good works come out of this is wonderful."

K.H. / **How do you measure your success?**

J.F. / We don't take it for granted.

K.H. / **What do you tell others who come to you seeking advice about starting a new career?**

J.F. / You want to make chocolate? Great! Do you like to wash dishes? Any business has day-to-day details that are repetitive in nature. So pick a profession where you can tolerate the grunt work the best. I really do like to measure! And I don't have a problem with dish detail.

K.H. / **Any resources you found helpful?**

D.L. / The Internet. Online chat groups and shopping online vendors for all the resources we need to fuel our passion.

J.F. / Our biggest resource was and is each other.

EDUCATIONAL "VACATIONS"

If you're interested in a new craft or trade, take a trip where you come home with more than a bunch of photos. Similar to VocationVacations, educational vacations are a great way to study with the masters.

Typically a week or two long, these intense training sessions with professionals allow you to accumulate experience while you are still working at your current job. They can be a great way to build the expertise and proficiency needed for a new career. They can be pricey, but far less than you might spend if you enrolled in a full-time degree program at a local college.

The sheer variety of offerings worldwide is mind numbing. Serious cooks might want to thumb through the Guide to Cooking Schools published by ShawGuides. It contains detailed descriptions of more than a thousand schools, colleges, culinary apprenticeships, cooking vacations, and wine programs worldwide. It's divided into two sections: one for career programs and one for recreational programs.

Want to become a bagpiper? There are two-week courses taught by world-class piper instructors at the North American Academy of Piping in Valle Crucis, North Carolina. Whet your woodcarving, quilting, or doll-making skills at Fletcher Farm School in Ludlow, Vermont, which offers five-day courses. You can also sign up for an arduous two-week course in carpentry, furniture building, landscaping, or stone masonry and learn to really build homes at Yestermorrow Design/Build School in Warren, Vermont.

WAYS TO PREPARE FOR NONPROFIT WORK

DON'T EXPECT TO BE WELCOMED WITH OPEN ARMS JUST BECAUSE YOU WERE SUCCESSFUL IN THE FOR-PROFIT WORLD. Seek out nonprofits looking for people with business experience, which can help the nonprofit achieve its goals. Know what you can do for the field you are getting into by having a complete understanding of the organization's goals and expectations.

BE REALISTIC ABOUT YOUR SALARY, VACATION, AND BENEFITS. Look at resources such as Salary.com to give you a sense of the salaries in the field you are looking at. Salaries tend to be 20 to 50 percent lower than in the for-profit world. Visit the Association for Fundraising Professionals site (www.afpnet.org) to learn more about compensation and other issues.

GET TRAINING. Credentials help in the nonprofit world, and there's a lot to learn. Importantly, a nonprofit degree or certificate can add $20,000 to $40,000 to earnings. A number of people complete a master's in social work in their fifties. There are roughly thirty programs that grant master's degrees in nonprofit study. (Many programs offer night courses, so with some effort, you can fit them into your existing work and personal life.) Many other programs offer degrees in public administration, philanthropic studies, and social work—some can even be earned completely online. For a listing of hundreds of undergraduate, graduate, and certificate programs, go to academic.shu.edu/npo. This is a detailed lineup compiled by Roseanne Mirabella, a professor at Seton Hall University. Some institutions that offer training include New York University

(Master of Science program in fundraising), Columbia University, Case Western Reserve University, Indiana University, Seton Hall, and the University of San Francisco. Course work includes nonprofit marketing, fundraising, campaigns, corporate philanthropy, ethics, and law.

KNOW YOURSELF. You need a certain amount of humility. Decisions are usually made by consensus, so if you are an independent operator, this might not be a good fit. You can't allow yourself to get discouraged easily. In the nonprofit world, you work hard, and there is usually never enough resources to make it all happen as quickly or successfully as you would want. And if you're a go-getter-make-things-happen-fast kind of worker, whoa—a nonprofit can test your patience to the nth degree.

CHECK OUT WEB SITES SUCH AS COMMONGOOD CAREERS (www .cgcareers.org) AND BRIDGESTAR (www.bridgestar.org). The sites help executives make transitions to nonprofits and is an excellent source for people with broad skill sets to shift into the nonprofit world. They list everything from volunteer opportunities to internships to board opportunities, as well as contacts for headhunters looking for those who can play executive roles in nonprofits.

A ROAD MAP FOR WOMEN IN RETIREMENT

▼

Charlotte Frank remembers heading downtown on a brilliant September morning toward her office in Lower Manhattan, where she was an executive with the Port Authority of New York and New Jersey.

She never made it. Her office was in the North Tower of the World Trade Center, and it was September 11, 2001. She couldn't get past Canal Street. She stood with dozens of onlookers and watched the first tower collapse. They uttered almost in unison, "Oh . . . my . . . God."

Frank retired the next year at sixty-seven, after helping the agency get back on its feet. "I was on my way out," she says. "But that precipitated it. You never know what's going to happen, so you'd better get on with what you really want to do—your next act."

She got on with it. Within days, she was working full time with no pay for the Transition Network, a New York nonprofit for women over fifty who are at or near retirement. Frank had founded the group two years earlier with her friend Christine Millen, then fifty-eight and a partner at the consulting firm Deloitte & Touche.

Frank and Millen had spent many lunches trying to sort out what to do with their own retirements. They came to realize that they were on the leading edge of a generation of women better educated and more ambitious than any before. These were the first women to have reached top-level positions in business, government, and other fields, and they were facing possibly thirty years of retirement—without a road map. "We asked ourselves: 'What do you do when you don't have a purpose? What do you do when you don't have your career? What do you do when you don't have your identity? Your social network?' It's a time of major loss."

Frank and Millen launched the fledgling outfit with no budget, staff, or office space—but with a firm belief that they were onto something big. The women broadly define retirement as a series of transitions—a bridge from one career to another or from employment to volunteerism, advocacy, or community—a grassroots movement that "reimagines retirement." The challenge was to build networking groups to provide support and share information. "I wanted to continue to have an impact on the world and needed an organizational structure to do so," Frank says. "I always felt I could change the world by taking on large issues and large groups of people."

Frank still thinks big. The Transition Network (TTN) now reaches over 5,200 women in fifty states through its online newsletter, memberships, and workshops and is continually opening new chapters. There are currently eight chapters, from New York to San Francisco. Members range in age from their late forties to eighty-plus. Some women are retired. Others work part time or full time.

Frank came of age as a feminist in an era when a woman was encouraged to get an education and use it—to further her husband's career. "My mother actually told me not to show my intelligence if I wanted to get a man," she laughs. That is one piece of advice Charlotte Frank wisely ignored.

LOOKING BACK

K.H. / **What did the transition mean to you personally?**

C.F. / I am driven by a compulsion to do something, usually something that helps society cope with its problems. I'm not driven by accumulating wealth—I never was. When I worked for the government, I probably made $100,000 less than I would have in the private sector. I am blessed with a really good pension, so I could pursue what really mattered to me.

K.H. / **Were you confident you were doing the right thing? Any second-guessing?**

C.F. / I didn't know anything about running an organization or business planning, but I always thought our direction was right. I knew we were onto something big.

I admit it was a struggle for the first five years to bring in money. Finally, it was too much. That's when we committed to an executive director and started running it like a business. It was a great learning experience, and we never looked back.

K.H. / **Would have you done anything differently?**

C.F. / Not really. I wish we could have afforded to hire a director sooner. It was only when things started exploding in terms of growth that we realized we needed to step back and start thinking about raising money. Is it through contributions? Grants? Dues?

K.H. / **What has been the biggest surprise or reward for you?**

C.F. / It is without a doubt the formation of the Caring Collaborative, a TTN New York City pilot project.

In 2006 I was diagnosed with cancer and had surgery to remove my thyroid gland. I suddenly lost my voice and couldn't catch my breath—my vocal chords had become paralyzed as a side effect of the surgery. I had no energy and no appetite. I was seventy-three years old, living in an apartment in midtown Manhattan, where I have been for more than twenty years, and had no family nearby. My friends helped me by bringing home-cooked meals, grocery shopping, and coming along to my doctors' appointments to take notes, be my advocate, and even help pick up prescriptions at the pharmacy. I would never have asked them to do all that, but they knew I needed help.

"We asked ourselves: 'What do you do when you don't have a purpose? What do you do when you don't have your career? What do you do when you don't have your identity?' It's a time of major loss."

I realized then that you have to learn how to use your network when you need it. Some people don't learn how to ask for help until it's almost too late. As we get older, we need each other even more.

The Caring Collaborative is like a time bank—jump-started with help from the Visiting Nurse Service of New York, a home-health nonprofit. Each member earns an hour of credit by volunteering to help another member in need. Those credits can be redeemed for help with health problems later.

In the first four months, over two hundred people signed up to help others. That has been extraordinary.

K.H. / **How did your preparation help you succeed?**
C.F. / I have always been in a state of learning and just kept on going after I retired. You must be in a constant state of learning to succeed.

K.H. / **What advice do you give to others about starting a second act?**
C.F. / You need to be engaged with people. Try to connect with a network of peers or a community. Don't try to figure out what's next alone. You really have to open up, even though you might feel vulnerable. You have to connect, and you have to develop relationships.

Look for interesting volunteer opportunities. Regardless of whether you retire late, take an early-retirement package, or are laid off, you have a chance to really change your life. Volunteering can really shape your second act. It might lead directly to a specific job, or it might lead to a vision of a job. In my case, it led to the founding of an organization.

TTN was my second act. The Caring Collaborative is my third act. I have no idea what my fourth act is going to be, but I have every intention of having one. In my fourth act, though, I am going to do things that are totally irresponsible because I have been totally responsible my entire life.

K.H. / **What books and resources do you recommend?**
C.F. / *Smart Women Don't Retire—They Break Free*, *Looking Forward*, and *An Optimist's Guide to Retirement*.

VOLUNTEER TOWARD YOUR SECOND ACT

Career change isn't easy, particularly if you have been entrenched in one field and, perhaps, even one company for two decades or more.

To figure out if a certain type of business or cause is all you dream it will be, give it a test run by signing on as an unpaid helper. In many cases, you can take a crack at a myriad of options before you leave your current employer. And yes, volunteering is a viable route to a full-time gig. It happens. The potential employer gets a chance to see what you have to offer, and you get a sneak peek inside to see if the organization suits you.

But working for that one group might not be your ultimate goal. You might just want to get the flavor of that type of work or an overview of the industry. If you yearn to be a landscape designer, for example, you might volunteer at your city's horticultural center or lend your hand to a grounds committee for a historical home or museum known for its gardens.

Either way, volunteering gets you out, networking, and open to new opportunities and experiences. It lets you get your hands dirty.

Before you sign on, here are some questions to consider:

- What kind of organization or company fits with the career field you are hoping to explore? Interested in getting into the music business? Volunteering as a docent at a performing arts center can get you backstage and face to face with performers and their entourage. Want to start your own winery? Volunteer to work at a local vineyard during harvest time or help pour in the tasting room. Love to cook? How about offering to be a sous-chef at a nearby restaurant, free of charge?

- What size organization would suit you? Do you prefer a small group with a narrow focus and fewer resources, but greater opportunity to make a difference? Or are you drawn to a larger organization, which might offer skilled training and more potential job openings but less hands-on work?

- How deep do you want to dig in? Do you want to be out in the field, working directly with people, or would you rather develop strategies in an office? How much time can you commit? Weekends? Full time?

- How long of a commitment do you want to make? If you're just getting started, it's wise to seek a project with a clear time frame of six months or less.

- Are you prepared to approach this as you would a paying job? That means pulling together a résumé, interviewing, and dedicating yourself to all the professional skills and expertise you have nurtured and developed throughout your career.

NETWORKING

One of the hidden opportunities of looking for second acts is the ability to tap into the network you have been creating over the years. Your experience means you have more resources to draw on than people in their twenties and thirties. Here's how to work it:

STAY UP-TO-DATE. Update your online profiles on LinkedIn, Facebook, or the professional networking site Xing to signal your new career track. Do a Web search through these networking sites to see if you know anyone who's already working in the field you're interested in.

TAP INTO YOUR ROLODEX. Send out a blast e-mail using a tool like Mail Merge in Microsoft Word to personalize each message. Let your friends and associates know that you are thinking of changing careers, quickly list some of your work background and expertise to date, and let them in on the direction you are heading.

ALUMNI POWER. Mine alumni associations to track down fellow grads—even if you haven't spoken to classmates in years, people tend to want to assist those who share a common background.

YOU CAN ASK FOR HELP WITHOUT BEING PUSHY. It's as simple as asking for an introduction to someone who works in your future arena— offer to treat the person to coffee or a drink in exchange for some helpful information or informally exchange e-mails if an in-person meeting is not in the cards. You might also ask for any leads on professional groups or job opportunities. Keep your requests short and sweet, and be grateful to anyone who responds.

BETSY WERLEY, EXECUTIVE DIRECTOR
THE TRANSITION NETWORK

After twenty-five years of plying her legal expertise, first at law firms and later at JPMorgan Chase, Betsy Werley was ready for a change. She took a deep breath and made the leap from corporate lawyer to a position as the executive director of the Transition Network, the New York City–based nonprofit whose aim is helping women over fifty make transitions—including career changes, family situations, or any life change. She was one month shy of her fiftieth birthday. "I thought, gee, I'm turning fifty," Werley says. "I'm not getting any younger. Go out and let that next big thing happen."

In reality, it didn't happen that fast. It evolved gradually over a period of five or six years as she focused on how to try something new. "I always thought about a job in the nonprofit world," she says. "Even when I was at JPMorgan Chase, I was involved in networking projects for women."

First, she began by looking for boards to get involved with as a volunteer. She joined the Financial Women's Association and in 2001 was named its president. "I wasn't necessarily planning a career in nonprofit work at the time, but I knew it would open up a lot of opportunities," she says.

Her involvement with the FWA, especially as president, was her catalyst. It led her to network with other women, primarily at JP Morgan Chase and at other nonprofits.

Having had a taste of leadership experience, she became convinced that she did want to work for a nonprofit and, importantly, for a much smaller organization.

So while Werley kept up her duties at JP Morgan Chase, she got busy prepping for her next act. She enrolled in courses at New York

University. She drafted up a new résumé. And she did the footwork. "I talked to a lot of people in the nonprofit world to understand where I might be a fit and see if my credentials made sense," she says. "Some of that was basic social networking," she says. Whether it was a party or professional function, Werley got out there and let people know what she was interested in.

And she hit the Internet. She surfed onto BoardnetUSA.org, a Web site for anyone looking for a nonprofit board. It's a single collection point for any board looking for new members to post its information. "It has a terrific search engine," Werley says. "Individuals can post where they are located, what kind of mission and organization they are looking for, and what their skill set is. Once you've posted your information, you get a weekly e-mail with a list of organizations looking for people who fit your profile."

At the same time, through the Financial Women's Association, she linked up with a couple of women who were doing consulting for nonprofit boards. "I told them about my interests, which were initially in two areas—using technology to enable people to solve problems, and women," she recalls.

She used her network to meet with people and say, "Here's the kind of organization I am looking for. Who do you know of and what's their reputation, and could you make an introduction?" Once she was in the door, Werley was able to talk with people doing the work she was interested in.

It was enlightening. "I learned about different kinds of jobs and different sizes of organizations, and had people in those jobs tell me about how they got there and talk to me about myself as a candidate for those organizations," Werley says. Bit by bit she narrowed down her choices.

Among the people she talked with were the founders Charlotte Frank and Christine Millen of the Transition Network, a group for women in circumstances much like her own. The tipping point came when her longtime employer offered her a buyout package of a year's salary, plus a year's benefits. It was her chance to make the break.

At the heart of it for Werley is the quest for meaning—which she believes comes in many different forms. "It can certainly be the mission of an organization," she says, "but I think meaning can also come from working for a smaller organization, where you make much more of a contribution. You don't feel you are a cog in a huge machine. And you have more control over what you are doing."

At the Transition Network, she was the second employee.

ANOTHER KIND OF REWARD

Most people wouldn't walk away from an eye-popping paycheck. But forty-eight-year-old Kim Ogden did. "It was time," she says with a gentle laugh.

After rising to become partner at Bain & Company, the Boston-based management consulting firm, she headed off at the end of 2002, after fourteen years. Her destination: an unpaid position as chief operating officer of Agape International, a nonprofit organization that cares for children in India—ages eighteen months to sixteen years—orphaned as a result of AIDS.

Ogden had harbored the altruistic goal of blending challenging work with giving back to society ever since she graduated from Dartmouth College, armed with a degree in economics. She did interview with nonprofit firms after earning an MBA from Harvard, but nothing met her salary objectives or offered the learning opportunity and responsibility she desired. "I figured I should pay off my student loans and be more effective later with some training," she says.

The years slid by, and with them came lucrative promotions—until 9/11. "I hit the wall," she remembers. "I realized I could die tomorrow. I had been feeling I wasn't really doing what I was supposed to be for a long time. I asked, 'Am I pleased with what

I have accomplished?' I had good intentions, but I wasn't actually doing anything to help those less fortunate."

In 2002 she took a six-month sabbatical. Ogden and her husband, Frank, also a management consultant, had socked away an ample nest egg. She began volunteering with a number of nonprofits, including the Boys & Girls Clubs of Boston. Then, a few months into her sabbatical, she heard Lynne Guhman speak at her church about her vision for AIDS orphanages. "We clicked right away," she remembers.

Guhman, also in her midforties, is another corporate expat. She first visited India in 2000 to help start an orphanage. There are an estimated 15.2 million AIDS orphans (children who have lost one or both parents to the epidemic) worldwide, according to the Henry J. Kaiser Family Foundation. Guhman became convinced that she could make a difference for tens of thousands of India's orphans—living in huge slums, their lives torn apart by AIDS. She quit her investment management job and returned to live in India.

Ogden heard Lynne speak and approached her at church. "I felt compelled to go talk to her about how I could help. We went out for coffee, and she described her vision for creating a nonprofit. She said she really needed someone to help on the U.S. side, setting up the organization and getting donors, and I immediately said, 'I'm your girl!'"

In 2003 Ogden helped Guhman launch Agape—pronounced "ah-guh-pay," which is the Greek word for unconditional love. In Hyderabad, a city in south-central India that has been ravaged by AIDS, Agape runs five orphanages, home to about 225 children, as well as a twenty-five-bed hospital. The group also runs its own school.

Today, Ogden is responsible for running all of Agape's U.S. operations out of her home office. Her corporate background provided a network of potential donors to call upon—some four hundred have signed on to date, in addition to private foundations. She handles everything from accounting to fundraising and licking stamps for handwritten thank-you notes, while also caring for two teenage boys and a five-year-old daughter.

Plans call for Agape to open one or two additional orphanages per year. Currently, two of the existing orphanages are designated for children who are HIV positive, and more will be added. "One-third of our kids are HIV positive themselves," says Ogden, who recently returned from a trip to India.

Ogden is always moved by meeting the kids she is helping. "These children just soak up the love," she says, on the edge of tears. "They just want to be held when they arrive, and before long, they are laughing, going to school, and playing with the other children."

Ogden admits to sometimes missing the instant respect afforded a partner at Bain. "I've had to let it go," she says. "There's something so liberating about not caring about that anymore." Without missing a beat, she cites Luke 12:48: "To whom much is given, much is expected."

—— Q & A ——

LOOKING BACK

K.H. / **What did this career move mean to you personally?**

K.O. / There is a generally understood "up or out" policy in management consulting. When I initially took the job, I did not expect to become a career consultant. But there I was, fourteen years later, a partner. I liked the work very much—I liked the problem solving, the challenge and intellectual stimulation of new industries and companies, the camaraderie and satisfaction of working with very bright people. I didn't love the travel and long hours, especially as a mother and wife, but I was able to work part time, which allowed me flexibility in my schedule.

For me, the catalyst was 9/11. It just reinforced for me that life is short, and you shouldn't put off dreams or change. For the first time, I knew with certainty that I wanted to do something else. I knew I wanted to help people more directly.

"I hit the wall. I realized I could die tomorrow. I had been feeling I wasn't really doing what I was supposed to be for a long time. I had good intentions, but I wasn't actually doing anything to help those less fortunate."

K.H. / **Were you confident and certain in what you were doing? Any second-guessing along the way?**

K.O. / In the past, when I'd thought about leaving Bain, there was always a lack of confidence and great uncertainty if it was the right thing to do. This time was different. I felt strongly that this was what I was supposed to do. The time was right. I miss the people at Bain very much, but I have never regretted the decision.

K.H. / **Anything you would have done differently?**

K.O. / I don't think so. I think for many who move on, there may be a thought that they should have done it earlier, but I don't regret the years I spent at Bain at all. I was happy there, and I learned a great deal that continues to serve me well.

K.H. / **What has been the biggest surprise? Unexpected rewards?**

K.O. / Working from home and working fewer hours allowed me to do a lot of things that I did not have time for before. I cherish the unplanned moments with my kids and my friends. I've been able to read a lot more and do a regular Bible study and a book club, which has added enormous richness to my life.

K.H. / **How big a role did potential financial rewards play in your decision to make a change?**

K.O. / None whatsoever. My new job is a net-negative proposition!

K.H. / **How did your preparation help you succeed?**

K.O. / The most important thing was having a supportive husband. Since I'd thought about leaving consulting fairly often, I had had many discussions with my husband about what that might mean financially and otherwise. He has always communicated that my happiness was primary—and that we would make any changes work.

K.H. / **What do you tell others who come to you for advice about following their passion or dream?**

K.O. / Do it! Life is short.

K.H. / **How do you measure your success?**

K.O. / This has changed a lot. Some of that change is certainly due to career change, but I'd also like to think I'm getting a little more mature. I no longer look to pay increases as a measure of success. Since I really don't have a boss or get any sort of structured feedback, it's also not a positive performance evaluation! I do have an objective measure of "my" success in the total donations to Agape—I think about success as the number of smiling kids I see when I go to our orphanages.

Getting away from an environment that was so intensely career focused has also helped me look at other parts of my life. Am I being a good mother? A good wife? A good friend? In the end, it's the depth of my relationships that matter.

K.H. / **Were there any books or resources you found helpful to you as you planned your second act?**

K.O. / The Bible helped a lot! Also, *The Purpose Driven Life*. I think even nonreligious people can connect with this advice, which is really to be what you were meant to be. And don't get distracted by the "things" of this world—in the end, they don't matter at all.

FUNDRAISING

If you have a great idea and have done all the legwork to start your nonprofit, this is where the rubber meets the road. How do you pay for it all? Fundraising is a key ingredient to your ultimate success and requires nurturing a rapport with donors, establishing a database of existing and potential donors, as well as attracting, training, and motivating volunteers. Other key aspects include writing grant proposals, overseeing e-mail and phone campaigns, and running fundraising events from galas to film screenings.

Here are three Web sites to help you learn the ropes and connect you with potential donors:

THE ASSOCIATION OF FUNDRAISING PROFESSIONALS (www.afpnet.org) represents over twenty-six thousand members in 171 chapters throughout the United States, Canada, Mexico, and China, working to advance philanthropy through training courses, advocacy, research, education, and certification programs.

THE FOUNDATION CENTER (www.foundationcenter.org) educates thousands of people each year through a full curriculum of training courses—in the classroom and online. Free and affordable classes nationwide cover the grant proposal writing and fundraising skills. The center also maintains databases of information on the more than ninety-five thousand foundations, corporate donors, and grant-making public charities in the United States and 1.3 million of their recent grants.

The site consists of a variety of free search tools, tutorials, downloadable reports, and other information updated daily, including *Philanthropy News Digest*, its daily news service, and PubHub, its searchable online collection of thousands of reports published by foundations and nonprofit organizations. It also publishes books ranging from basic primers on fundraising to nonprofit management.

The site ChangingthePresent.org allows nonprofits to raise awareness of their work and helps connect nonprofits with people seeking to make gift donations. It also features a tool for conducting fundraising drives to support a variety of causes.

TAKE A COURSE IN FUNDRAISING

One way to sharpen your fundraising skills is to enroll in classes offered by the Foundation Center and the Association of Fundraising Professionals (AFP).

The AFP's Essentials of Fundraising series offers introductory-level sessions—five three-hour interactive workshops—to introduce the novice fundraiser to the fundamental concepts and techniques of fundraising. Volunteers, too, will find the Essentials of Fundraising helpful in learning how to approach potential donors for contributions.

Here are some areas the workshops cover:

- Starting a development program

- Identifying and soliciting annual donors

- Seeking grant support

- Developing a board and volunteer base

- Securing individual major gifts

The workshops allow you to develop skills that can be customized to fit your organization. Moreover, you'll have the opportunity to network and develop relationships with other fundraisers in your area. And there are plenty of take-away tools such as sample fundraising plans, solicitation letters, policies, and guidelines to jumpstart your efforts.

TEN TIPS TO GET YOU SPEAKING LIKE A PRO

Since 1924 Toastmasters International has helped many people from all walks of life increase their speaking skills and self-confidence in front of an audience. Toastmasters has nearly 235,000 members in 12,036 clubs in 106 countries. Most meetings consist of approximately twenty people who meet weekly for an hour or two. Participants practice and learn skills of effective speech: focus, organization, language, vocal variety, and body language.

Here are Toastmaster's top ten ways to help rein in those stomach butterflies and give smooth, self-assured presentations:

1. KNOW YOUR MATERIAL. Be familiar with more about your topic than you include in your speech. Use humor, personal stories, and conversational language—that way you won't easily forget what to say.

2. PRACTICE. PRACTICE. PRACTICE. Rehearse out loud with all equipment you plan on using. Revise as necessary. Work to control filler words, such as "like," "um," and "you know." Practice pausing and breathing during your speech. Practice with a timer and allow time for the unexpected.

3. KNOW THE ROOM. Arrive early, walk around the speaking area, and practice using the microphone and any visual aids.

4. KNOW THE AUDIENCE. Greet some of the audience members as they arrive. It's easier to speak to a group of friends than to strangers.

5. RELAX. Begin by addressing the audience. It buys you time and calms your nerves. Pause, smile, and count to three before saying anything. Transform nervous energy into enthusiasm.

6. VISUALIZE YOURSELF GIVING YOUR SPEECH. Imagine yourself speaking, your voice loud, clear, and confident. Visualize the audience clapping—it will boost your confidence.

7. REALIZE THAT PEOPLE WANT YOU TO SUCCEED. Audiences want you to be interesting, stimulating, informative, and entertaining. They're rooting for you.

8. DON'T APOLOGIZE FOR ANY NERVOUSNESS OR PROBLEM. The audience probably never noticed it.

9. CONCENTRATE ON THE MESSAGE—NOT THE MEDIUM. Focus your attention away from your own anxieties and concentrate on your message and your audience.

10. GAIN EXPERIENCE. Mainly, your speech should represent you—as an authority and as a person. Experience builds confidence, which is the key to effective speaking. A Toastmasters club can provide the experience you need in a safe and friendly environment.

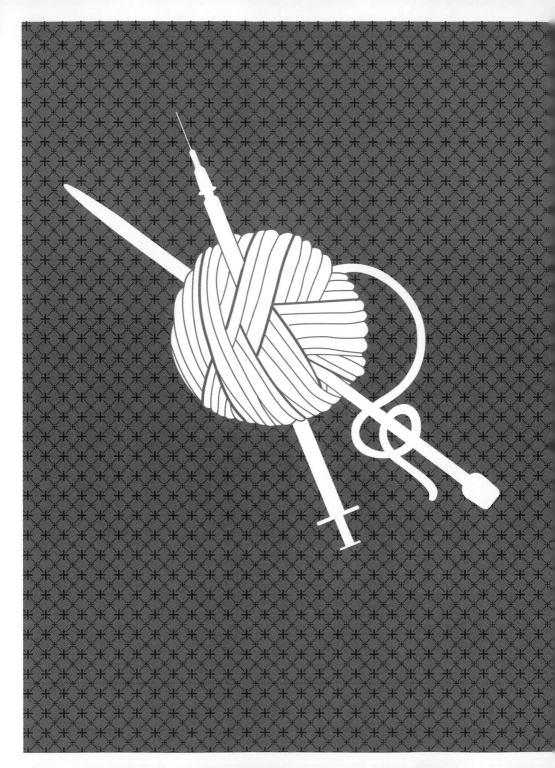

STITCHING TOGETHER
A NEW LIFE

▼

Susan Wolcott is a child of the '60s. As soon as she graduated from high school in 1969, she left her hometown of Olympia, Washington, and "did the hippie thing," she says, taking the time to find out what was important to her—community, listening, spirituality, holistic health, creativity, the environment.

She found a profession that reflected those values: nursing. It felt right. "Nursing to me meant kindness and compassion for human beings," says Wolcott. For twelve years, she worked as a clinical nurse in hospices, home care, hospitals, and rehabilitation and outpatient clinics. Eventually, she moved into higher-paying managerial positions at managed-care companies and software firms specializing in health care.

But as health care began to be driven more by insurance and less by patient care, Wolcott became disillusioned. She kept her day job but went back to school, earning a master's degree in social and organizational learning from George Mason University in Fairfax, Virginia, where she had relocated with four adopted children after her divorce. In 2002 she started moonlighting as a life coach, helping people deal with personal and professional transitions. While coaching others, she realized she needed to make some changes of her own.

"My earliest memory is the peaceful sound of my mother's knitting needles clicking together," says Wolcott, who began knitting at nine. She had recently picked the needles up again, after a sixteen-year hiatus, during a weekend in Santa Fe with her mother and two sisters. "I soon found that in a tense or tired moment, knitting a few rows brought me back to calmness and centeredness," she says.

Before long, she and her sister Jill, an avid knitter and knitwear designer in San Francisco, had started a side business called Y2Knit, a series of teaching retreats. It hit the market just as the knitting boom was taking off. According to the Craft Yarn Council of America, the number of women ages forty-five and younger who knit regularly has doubled since 1998, to almost one in five. "Knitting relaxes people by giving them something to focus on," Wolcott says. As their workshop business grew, Jill began designing patterns for Y2Knit to sell.

Meanwhile, while scoping out a location for a retreat, Wolcott had an odd but good feeling. Driving through the rolling Maryland farmland seventy miles northwest of Washington, D.C., she sensed that this could be home.

It was then she decided to quit her job as a director with an online physician-patient communications network and buy a place in the country. It would be both home and yarn store. "It hit me with a total assurance," she recalls. She was over fifty and felt a "deepening of this desire to do something that was meaningful and purposeful."

She eventually landed in quaint Funkstown, Maryland, as the owner of a . . . well . . . funky, pink log house dating back to 1780. In the summer of 2003, Wolcott opened the brightly painted Y2Knit retail shop.

Today Y2Knit is in the black. It has an active client list of five thousand knitters and a growing number of retail yarn shops that carry its pattern line. Wolcott covers her rent and living expenses, though she earns only about a quarter of her last job's pay. "My change was about lifestyle," she says.

The rewards have been plentiful. She is her own boss, operates in a creative world, and buys much of her food from local farmers. She has no commute to work. Her fifteen-year-old Honda is usually parked in the driveway.

More important, the entrepreneurial venture has reconnected Wolcott with the altruistic values that had originally led her to nursing. "I have a ministry," she says. "Not in a religious way, but it's about ministering to people and meeting their needs." Connecting people with resources fills her days. Women stop by to talk about kids, spouses, recipes, job interviews, movies, dreams, and frustrations.

"I have no regrets about giving up the paycheck," Wolcott says. "My life is not about money—it's about my spirit."

—— Q & A ——
LOOKING BACK

K.H. / **What did the transition mean to you personally?**
S.W. / It was about being really true to what I believe. As we go through life, we often make choices that are best because our parents want us to, or because society wants us to, because it's best for our children. Those aren't wrong choices necessarily, but they are the things that impact our choices. This was a chance for me to make choices totally based on what my soul wanted.

K.H. / **Were you confident and certain about what you were doing? Any second-guessing?**
S.W. / I didn't have a lot of second-guessing. Sometimes I'd wake up and think, what the heck am I doing? But I really didn't have doubts.

It felt very much like this was totally going to work out. Once I'd moved, I realized I was living in a very conservative Bible Belt area, which was a little challenging for me because that is not who I am. There were times when I would meditate for two hours in the morning, focusing on affirmations.

Now all it takes is a couple quick words to myself to know that this is going to turn out okay.

K.H. / **Anything you would have done differently?**
S.W. / I don't know that I can go there. There is nothing big that sticks out in my mind.

K.H. / **What has been the biggest surprise or unexpected reward?**
S.W. / The wonderful people I've met and discovered and then the well-spring within myself that has come out. People who have known me throughout my entire life would say I am a strong person. That has manifested itself in new ways in this career. I almost hate to say it because I find it really trite, but this is where I am supposed to be.

K.H. / **How did the potential financial rewards play in your decision to make the transition?**
S.W. / It is not a part of it. It was never about the money.

K.H. / **How did your preparation help you succeed?**
S.W. / I took it slowly. My preparation had a lot to do with building up my inner resources and developing a strong sense of self. I kept doing these positive affirmations. They helped me prepare and still do.

And then having an external support system is key. I have that. My children are supportive. My mother, who is eighty-six, is very supportive, and so are my friends.

My education also helped build my confidence. My graduate degree in social and organizational behavior added to my tool kit. I am probably overeducated for what I am doing, or some people might perceive that. But I couldn't do what I am doing without that added education. It gave me a stronger sense of self—really empowered me.

At the same time, it also provided me with the technical knowledge about business organization, how to run a meeting professionally, and how to write a great business plan. As I work within this industry, it really helps to have that grounding; it continually helps me as I create and grow the business.

Coaching was also a focus of my education and preparation for this new stage. I studied with the Coaches Training Institute and co-taught a class after graduation in group dynamics. Today, I coach formally, as well as pretty much all the time with people; even teaching knitting is like coaching somebody. So I feel like I gained some really wonderful skills there that have made me a really great teacher.

K.H. / **What do you tell others who come to you seeking advice about making a career change and following their passion or a dream?**
S.W. / I tell them that if it is burning in you, in my belief, you absolutely need to follow it. You're not serving yourself, or anybody, if you don't.

I think you do have to make sure there is water in the pool and that it is deep enough. You can't just jump off the end of the dock. You can't abandon everything and jump into a new field without some preparation. It may mean a transition period where you need to build up financial security or learn a new skill set, but you can certainly start trying to figure it out and take small steps.

Don't start a small business without a clear, solid business plan. Make sure that it's a written business plan. It is really important to write these things down so they are not just ideas in your head. Know what you are going to do. Have what-if scenarios. What if you don't make as much money as you think you're going to?

Our plan is a comprehensive one. First, we have several lines of business. I think the reason we have succeeded is it is not just the store—it's also the line of patterns and events. We have a combination of things.

"I have no regrets about giving up the paycheck. My life is not about money— it's about my spirit."

Second, part of our business plan is a strong marketing approach. You have to know how you are going to sell your product and services. Our Web site is a big part of that. If you don't have a Web site, no one is going to take you seriously. You can create the Web site yourself or you can pay somebody to do it. You need to keep it current, though. We just redid our Web site to better reflect us.

Once you know where you are heading, review the plan at set intervals. Jill and I got together a few weeks ago because our plan had some holes in it. It had weakened. It's really easy to start using bubble gum to patch up the holes—but we needed to reevaluate the way we were doing things.

It's important to network with people in the field you are entering. We are very active in our trade association. Even though we are a small business with two people, we make the time. We're both on Twitter! Jill has more followers than I do. I had said, "I'm not going there . . . it's just one more thing." I resisted. I have to force myself to stay up with the new technology and social networking.

I tell people to seek out a career coach, and not just because I studied it. I think it's a good idea for many people going through a career change. Coaching is like therapy. There are times when you need it. There's nothing wrong with it. I invite people who are interested in starting a knit shop to come for a personal retreat here, to come spend a day here.

K.H. / **Are there any books or resources that were helpful to you?**
S.W. / Cheryl Richardson's *Life Makeovers: Take Time for Your Life*, and Barbara Sher's *I Could Do Anything If I Only Knew What It Was.*

K.H. / **How do you measure your success?**
S.W. / I do have measurements. They are not crystal clear all the time. One of them is: do I get out of bed in the morning and look forward to the day ahead? I think we all have had that experience.

Part of the success that I measure is the incredible interactions with people, and I have them several times a week, where I see some kind of transformation in them. It could be as simple as, oh, they now get their knitting project. More often, it is something deeper within their lives that somehow has happened as a result of that project, a little "aha" moment. Very often they say, "I am so glad you are here." And that's how I measure my success.

And certainly the fact that I can pay the rent and bills every month.

CONNECTING WITH A CAREER COACH

If you know you need a change but are unsure of what to do, a career coach can help you set goals, clearly outline the steps to take you there, and motivate you to make it happen. Hiring the right person to guide you along on this personal journey is not simple and takes legwork. There are countless career coaches touting their services with a variety of styles and philosophies, and winnowing down the field requires doing some due diligence. Here are some smart ways to find someone who is qualified:

LOOK FOR QUALIFICATIONS. Career coaching is a self-regulated industry and emerging profession. Many coaches have been doing it for years without adding professional designations. But designations are a sign of some formal training and of adherence to general standards of professionalism. Look for one who is certified by a trade group like the nonprofit International Coach Federation (ICF) (www.coachfederation.org). The ICF is the only organization that awards a global credential, which is currently held by over 4,800 coaches worldwide. ICF-credentialed coaches have met stringent educational requirements, received specific coach training, and achieved a designated number of experience hours, among other requirements. An additional search link is the Association of Career Professionals (www.acpinternational.com). Accredited career counselors located by state can also be found in the directory of the National Career Development Association (www.ncda.org).

EXPLORE THE PAST CAREER PATH OF A POTENTIAL COACH. Many so-called career coaches are more life coaches, who focus on esoteric life choices and may lack practical work world advice. Find out as much as you can about their career path, both in the coaching field and in the regular work world. It's even better if they have been through a career transition or have a track record of working with people going through the process. Don't be bashful about questioning potential coaches on their level of expertise for your particular needs.

ASK FOR AT LEAST THREE REFERENCES. Of course, no one is going to hand over names of clients to call who didn't love them, but this is an important step in your process. You never know what you might learn when you get someone on the phone. Plus, it's imperative to know a potential coach's work style and how he or she succeeded with other clients starting a new career.

SAY NO TO GROUP SESSIONS. Find a coach who conducts one-on-one sessions. These can be in person, by phone, or by e-mail, but you want their full attention. Phone sessions are commonplace these days, which in many ways is to your advantage. You aren't restricted to signing on with a coach in your town, and you don't waste time getting to and from meetings and making small talk.

EXPECT A FREE INITIAL CONSULTATION. Once you've narrowed your search, you'll want to interview a few candidates. Never agree to work with a coach without a trial run. This initial session should be gratis. If there is a charge for this meet and greet, pass.

ASK ABOUT FEES. Rates vary significantly, anywhere from $50 to $400 per hour. Some coaches require a minimum number of hours.

On average, coach-client relationships last from six months to a year. You might sign on for one or two meetings to jump-start your new career course, or an arrangement with weekly or monthly meetings might suit your needs. Some coaches will provide resources such as books and give homework assignments to prepare for future sessions.

CHECK OUT THE COACH'S WEB SITE. This should give you insight into the coach's areas of expertise and what he or she has published. Search the coach's name on the Web and see if you find uncensored comments written by other clients.

KNOW THE DIFFERENCE BETWEEN A LIFE AND CAREER COACH. A career coach hones in on career issues—transition, choices, growth, and development. A life coach, though not a therapist, typically deals with broader areas—relationships, stress-reduction, and personal growth—and then helps you get unstuck or move through fears. A life coach can specialize in careers and might be helpful especially if your new direction will require significant personal change.

GET A WRITTEN AGREEMENT. This is a business relationship, so treat it like one with a formal agreement that defines the duties of each party. Verbal agreements can be risky and leave both the client and the coach susceptible to unexpected misunderstandings.

By working through these steps, you have a good chance of hiring a reputable coach. But there is one more thing. It comes down to something intangible: a human connection. You'll be doling out private details of your life, your dreams, and your strengths and weaknesses with your coach. You have to trust the coach and feel comfortable laying it all before him or her. This is scary stuff, and you need a steady hand to hold from time to time.

Ultimately, the career coach you hire should inspire you, push you, and give you the inner confidence to step into the unfamiliar with the grace and strength that comes from knowing deep inside that you are on the right path.

LEARNING LIFE'S LESSONS

On the day of his ex-business partner's funeral, Cliff Stevenson found a flier stuck in his door. It was an ad for a teaching degree at a nearby college. And it struck a nerve.

Stevenson had harbored a desire to teach since his undergraduate days at the University of Pennsylvania. But when he saw only a handful of upperclassmen getting teaching jobs, he dropped the master's of education program he'd been eyeing and earned bachelor's degrees in economics and history. Later, he returned to Penn for an MBA from Wharton. In 1981 a job in real-estate finance and mortgage banking landed him a lucrative career in Pittsburgh.

Just two weeks before the funeral in 1996, Stevenson's dying partner had asked, "So what are you going to do with your life, Stevo? You said you weren't going to do this mortgage thing forever."

For Stevenson, fifty-five, that early death, combined with the sudden death of his brother at age forty-three not long before, was a life-changing event. "You never know what's going to happen in life," he says. "I knew it was the right time to do something different."

So he chucked his twenty-year career to follow his heart. For the past seven years, Stevenson has been teaching social studies to eighth graders and high school students in the Hampton Township School District in Allison Park, outside Pittsburgh. His salary is about one-sixth of what he made in his best years as a mortgage banker. "I didn't want to get to seventy-five and ask, what did I do with my life? I financed and sold real estate," says Stevenson. "I want to give back, to have an effect on somebody."

Self-confident and disciplined, Stevenson also benefited from the full support of his wife, Diane, who earns a solid income as a regional merchandise manager for Macy's. The couple has no children. They sold their century-old Victorian home outside Pittsburgh for twice what they paid, downsizing to a smaller town-house on up-and-coming Washington's Landing, an island in the Allegheny River, within spitting distance of Pittsburgh's downtown Golden Triangle. Now they don't have a mortgage.

Next, Stevenson went back to school. For two years before he resigned from his firm, he took night courses to get a master's degree in education at Duquesne University. Since he had an undergraduate degree in history, all he needed were seven additional courses in education to be certified as a social studies teacher in Pennsylvania.

That said, he still had to wait for a job to open. His first year was spent working a $5,000-stipend internship at a local school district, followed by another two years as a substitute teacher. Then in 2002 he was hired at Hampton.

In many ways, his twenty years of corporate deal making gives Stevenson an edge. He's teaching his students skills they need for life—how to write effectively, speak confidently in public, and solve problems under pressure.

Surprisingly, he works more hours than he did in his old career—arriving at school by 7A.M., he shuttles between two schools, where he teaches a total of four courses per day and 158 students—and wraps up his workday around 6:30. He goes home, cooks dinner, and heads upstairs to his office for a couple of hours of grading papers and preparing for the next day's classes.

The payback is a passion for his work, a better night's sleep, and improved health. Stevenson also feels intellectually stimulated by teaching timely topics and current affairs. And, of course, the feedback he gets from his pupils can't be measured: "I'm always amazed when a student e-mails me from college, thanking me for pushing them to do their best. You never know when you've touched someone."

—— Q & A ——

LOOKING BACK

K.H. / **What did the career transition mean to you personally?**

C.S. / I came to Pittsburgh when I was thirty years old. I was hired by a mortgage banking company here, and it required a lot of selling. I'm not really a cold-call seller. I saw myself doing that for ten years but no more.

When I got to be forty, I realized I was halfway through my life, and I thought, okay, what have I done? We didn't have kids. My wife had a decent job, and we're not very materialistic. The need for money was not the issue. I knew we would always be able to feed ourselves and cover our medical bills.

I tell my seniors the last day of class about the triangle of life—body, mind, and soul. You have to keep those things in balance.

I realized that there has got to be more to life then just going to work and bringing home good money and buying nice stuff. Before you die, you want to be able to say you made a difference—maybe not in the world, but in somebody else's life.

K.H. / **Were you confident in what you were doing? Any second-guessing along the way?**

C.S. / I didn't have any second-guessing about becoming a teacher. I did second-guess about my ability to get a job.

"I didn't want to get to seventy-five and ask, what did I do with my life?"

K.H. / **How did your preparation help you succeed?**

C.S. / I started planning years before I switched careers. My wife and I thought carefully about the financial aspects. When I decided I wanted to make this move, I set a target date for when I would leave my mortgage banking business. That allowed me to go to school at night on the sly and pick up my education degree over a two-year period. I would take a course a semester while continuing to work for two full years, trying to stuff away as much money as I could.

I left when I was forty-four. I figured if I waited too long, I would get to the point where I was too old.

I was also patient. I was able to pave my way through the internship program that exists for teachers in Pennsylvania. It's a one-year internship where you work for a school, and they pay you $5,500, using you as a sub. I did that for a year and continued to sub for another two years. Then when Hampton hired me, I worked half time for two years.

I made a backup plan. As I was going to get my education degree, I was also taking classes to become a financial planner in case I couldn't find work as a teacher. I have an MBA in finance from Wharton, so I knew about money management. To be a planner, you had to take five specific courses on taxes and insurance to be nationally certified.

We downsized and simplified our lives. We wanted to change our lifestyle and get reinvigorated. We loved our house, but it was a hundred-year-old house with an acre of land. Every weekend there were four or five chores to be done. I like to do that stuff myself, but it was too much. Moving to the two-bedroom condo freed up a lot of time.

K.H. / **Anything you would have done differently?**
C.S. / I don't think so.

K.H. / **What has been the biggest surprise or unexpected reward of making this move for you?**
C.S. / The thing I like about teaching is you can never be good enough. You can always be better. It is challenging and always will be. The most positive thing I get is the feedback from the kids. I get letters from kids the year after they graduate, saying, "I want to thank you. Your class was the most college-like class I took in high school. You were tough, but I'm glad I had you." That's what's in it for me.

K.H. / **How big a role did financial rewards play in your decision to make a career transition?**
C.S. / None. I've been teaching full time for seven years now. When we bought this condo, we put on a minimum mortgage to get some tax write-off. When you don't have big mortgages or credit card debt or car loans, you can live on far less income.

K.H. / **What do you tell others who come to you for advice about following their passions or their dreams?**
C.S. / Think about what you enjoy and what you might want to do ahead

of time. I began by taking a half-day class at a community college that cost $40. It was a chance to spend time evaluating myself through a self-analysis course designed to identify my abilities, values, and interests. You take the tests over three hours and then graph the results together. Where they intersect, you find careers you might consider. It got me thinking: Do you want to work alone or with people? Flexible hours or set ones?

Read *Zen and the Art of Making a Living*. It's a self-analysis book about finding what is meaningful to you and what you really want to do.

Don't worry if you don't know immediately what it is you want to do in your next career. Initially, I hadn't thought about teaching. I thought I would need to take far too many courses to get accredited. Then I found out that in Pennsylvania, with my economic and history degree, I only had to take seven specific courses mandated by the state. It wasn't until I got that brochure in the mail the day of the funeral that the light went on. I don't know if I would have ever thought about it.

Be a good Boy Scout; be prepared. Think hard about the financial aspects. Make sure you have the support of your spouse or partner. Have a plan, a timetable. I was clear: I'm going to go to school at night. I'm going to cover seven courses in two years. I had a backup plan, to be a financial planner, if it didn't work out. And I knew I would have to sub for a period of time.

Be pragmatic. It's good to have a passion—mine might have been to play major league baseball—but that's never going to happen! You have to do what your abilities and your personality are. You have to be honest with yourself. Know your strengths and weaknesses. Take the time to analyze yourself. Do the self-reflection. I am a very reflective person.

I'm not a risk taker. I'm a calculated-risk taker.

K.H. / **How do you measure your success?**

C.S. / I ask myself, "Do I feel good about it?" And I do. The kids tell me they're glad they had me for a teacher. Parents come up to me and thank me. I would be worried if I wasn't getting that kind of feedback. It makes me think I am doing it the right way. Deep inside I recognize and appreciate that I'm doing something for my soul—it gets me up in the morning. Teaching is a gift. I'm fortunate. It has truly brought the second half of my life into balance.

PREPARE YOURSELF

The secret to a successful second career begins with knowing who you are and where your talents will shine. Many of us know we want and need to keep working. Yet we're a little unsure of what work we're best suited to do. Finding the best job can be a soul-searching undertaking.

If you're not sure where you want to go, it's okay. Pause and allow yourself the time to make a frank evaluation of your skills and interests. Much of what you already know is transferable to your next pursuit, but it will take some self-exploration to see what truly suits you and your background. The key is to match your job or career to your interests and personality.

To help get you started, check out the free self-assessment quizzes at CareerPath.com's and Monster.com's career advice section. Career assessment tests rank among the most popular methods used to research a new job (in addition to exploring Web sites and consulting with friends and family, former coworkers, and others in the industry).

Two things to keep in mind:

- Don't expect a career assessment to point you to your future job per se. The results are merely suggestions based on that one area of assessment.

- Give honest answers. If you consciously or subconsciously answer questions to fit a preconceived outcome you have in mind, the results will not be very useful.

These career assessment tools provide a broad view of your interests, abilities, and personal values—all of which play an integral role in job choices and, ultimately, your job satisfaction. Gaining an awareness of occupational and personal temperaments, study habits, and job values can lead to meaningful and informed decision making. The expectation, of course, is that the results open up a variety of options to explore for a career shift and give you important insight into your working style to help you find the best fit.

FROM HIGH FINANCE
TO RAVIOLI

▼

It's a sunny Sunday in September, and Tim Sheerer is not on the golf course with his fifteen-year-old son, Johnny, playing in the annual father-son tournament. Instead, he's spending the day preparing meals for roughly 350 customers at la Cappella, an Italian bistro, in a Pittsburgh suburb. That's the restaurant he owns and operates with his wife, Colleen. The cook has called in sick.

Sheerer, forty-eight, is okay with that. Missing the golf outing is disappointing, but it's a rarity. In the six years since he traded in a $500,000-a-year Wall Street salary to start his own restaurant, he has spent many hours with his four kids, ages thirteen to nineteen, at various sporting events.

After graduating with an MBA from the University of Chicago, Sheerer spent over thirteen years rising through the ranks of Merrill Lynch's U.S. Money Market Group, specializing in short-term corporate debt. He worked a crazy schedule—one day in London, the next Milwaukee. Colleen was in charge of the kids and hugged the sidelines at their games. "I wasn't able to be there for them," Sheerer says.

Sports and family mean a lot to Sheerer. But he pressed on year after year for one more whopping January bonus—skipping the

BMW, sailboat, and second home. In time, the couple saved enough to leave investment banking and head to Pittsburgh, his hometown.

The idea to move back home started to take shape in the spring of 2001, when Tim's father, who had nearly died from a heart attack some sixteen years earlier, underwent quadruple bypass surgery. Then came the 9/11 terrorist attacks. Tim was not working in the World Financial Center that day, but the couple knew several people who died as the twin towers crumbled.

One month later, Tim turned forty. "I looked around, and I wanted more," he says. The couple asked themselves what meant most to them. The answer was simple: family.

While the couple belonged to a gourmet-cooking club, the notion of operating their own Italian restaurant never crossed their minds. It just worked out that way. Tim's sister knew of a new restaurant franchise venture moving into the Pittsburgh area. Intrigued, Tim signed on and eventually leased retail space. He spent a year working in one of the chain's existing suburban restaurants. He bused tables, washed dishes, sautéed, and more. "If I was going to ask someone else to do these jobs, I had to know how to do them myself," he says. Ultimately, Sheerer extricated himself from the franchise operator, opted to open an independent restaurant, and named it la Cappella, or the Chapel, for the Fox Chapel community many of its customers live in.

Tim's energetic entrepreneurial spirit and business and finance background, combined with Colleen's people skills, have made the effort rewarding. Restaurant regulars call Colleen the "ambassador" of the cozy, 110-seat dining establishment, which is tucked alongside a heavily trafficked strip mall. Three of the couple's kids work as busers, hosts, and waiters. It's a family affair.

Although eighty-hour weeks were standard early on for Tim, today the schedule is not so demanding. If one of the kids has a game, Tim will be there, oftentimes coaching. With four college tuitions in sight, la Cappella will have to show more of a profit in time. But for now, with a lower cost of living, no mortgage payment, and savings to tap, the couple has a cushion.

Tim's dad, now nearing seventy-three, has also been able to see almost every one of his grandchildren's games since the family moved to Pittsburgh. "You can't put a price on that," says Tim.

"And then we look at our children," says Colleen. "They're happy and thriving." Tim nods in agreement. "They're our legacy. We made this move for them and their future," he says as he heads back to the kitchen.

— Q & A —
LOOKING BACK

K.H. / **What did the transition mean to you personally?**

T.S. / A couple things happened. As a result of 9/11, I felt a major loss. I saw people I worked with pass away. In the Merrill Lynch grind, you go through every day, and you work, work, work, but that made me realize, hey, you only live once.

That tragedy, combined with my dad's bypass surgery, got us thinking about a change. When Colleen and I moved to New York, we thought we would only be there for five years, but we never re-evaluated it. Those two events caused us to really sit down and say, we're making a lot of money, but is this really where we want to be? Is this really what we want to do? Is this where we want the kids to grow up? If we don't talk about it now, ten years will go by like that, and we're past the point where we can really consider a move.

I was working a zillion hours, and I was starting to miss things with the kids that my brothers in Pittsburgh were able to do. My brother complained he wasn't making enough money, but he was coaching all his kids' sports teams. I couldn't even see my daughter play in a softball game because I was either out of town or still in the office.

K.H. / **Were you confident in what you were doing? Any second-guessing along the way?**

T.S. / I was going into a big unknown. I definitely second-guessed it— more often at two in the morning, when I was lying awake in bed. When you are plowing through the day, there is really no time for second-guessing. But when you wake up in the middle of the night, that's when you question, is this the right move?

K.H. / **Is there anything you would have done differently?**

T.S. / I would have taken more time. I was anxious to get going. I needed to slow down and do my due diligence. I just kept saying, yeah, this is perfect for me.

I relied on the franchise experts to tell me about certain things. At that point, I was not an authority on the restaurant business, so I trusted their advice. At the same time, though, there were four or five things about the design of the restaurant and purveyors that my gut told me to do differently.

But going the franchise route gave me enough confidence that I could get into the restaurant business successfully. I don't think I would have been comfortable leaving Merrill Lynch and opening up my own ma-and-pa restaurant without that interim move. I would have thought it was too big of a step. And as a result, when I opened my own restaurant, I was better prepared.

K.H. / **What have been the unexpected surprises or rewards of your second act?**

T.S. / The biggest surprise was not a good one. I planned to tap into my Merrill Lynch stock options as a financial cushion when needed. I thought I was in good shape with those to help us weather the storm in the restaurant the first couple of years. Then in 2008 my investment portfolio basically dried up. A few years ago, Merrill Lynch stock was $100; now it's trading around $13.

I learned it's important to go back and look at your investments. Are they safe? Obviously, in my case, the last two years they weren't safe. That was something I did not foresee and didn't contemplate. Merrill Lynch has been around forever.

We expected the restaurant part to be tough, but we didn't expect all the money we had saved to disappear in one fell swoop. We wake up and look at each other and say, well, we have our health, and the kids are all healthy.

A more positive reward is having time with the kids. First, we have them helping out in the restaurant. Colleen and I love it. The kids and the workers all know each other, and the employees are involved in the kids' lives. They actually care whether Johnny hits a home run in the game. And the fun part is I get to spend a lot more time with them. If I were still on Wall Street, Molly would be going to college at Penn State this year, and I don't know how well I would know her. Now I can go shopping with her for prom dresses.

K.H. / **How big a role did financial rewards play in your decision to make a change?**

T.S. / None. In fact, it was the opposite. I think in some cases, people have a job and make a career change because they want to make more money or need to make more money. For me, the money was good at Merrill Lynch, but the other aspects of the job weren't. I had done it for a long time, and I wasn't getting the reward out of the job that I used to get. In fact, I was getting kind of cynical about it because I was missing opportunities to do things with my family and my kids.

I moved to this new career knowing upfront that I wouldn't be able to make anywhere near the amount of money I used to make. Sometimes you have to measure financial rewards versus other rewards and decide what's more important.

K.H. / **How did your preparation help you succeed?**
T.S. / Most of my preparation was on-the-ground training. I trained for six months at another franchisee's restaurant before mine opened. I went in from 8 A.M. to 8 P.M. and did everything. I wanted to really understand what all the workers go through.

In a restaurant, a lot of owners stay out front, and they'll point at the kitchen and jokingly say, "That's my executive chef's field; I don't go back there." Not me. I can break down a dish machine. I sauté.

Last night, it was a cold, rainy Tuesday night, and we expected it to be slow, but the restaurant filled up; we had a fifteen-minute wait for tables. It was crazy. I went back in the kitchen where the executive chef and cooks were getting killed. I left Colleen up front, and I basically cooked for an hour to relieve the pressure. I can do that.

The second piece of my preparation that has been invaluable—securing the support of my family before I started. I had been successful in my first career, and the family trusted me. No one second-guessed me. The first couple of weeks in the restaurant, I was so busy, I couldn't even see straight, and I was thinking, oh my God, I don't know if I can do this kind of thing. My youngest brother and my sister came in and went to work. They bartended. They bussed tables. They did it without me even asking.

K.H. / **What advice do you give others who seek your advice about following their passion or their dream?**
T.S. / Don't jump in too fast. Do your due diligence. Take time to do what it is you want. I know it is very much a cliché, but you only live

once. I say that phrase a lot to Colleen and the kids. There are too many times that you hear that people don't do something, and then five, ten, fifteen years later, they regret it. You must stop and really say, what are my goals? I think most of us live our lives without goals, or at least you don't sit down and put them on paper.

I don't know too many people who write down the pros and cons of their decisions. We did. We measured all that.

"We look at our children. They're happy and thriving. They're our legacy. We made this move for them and their future."

K.H. / **How do you measure your success?**

T.S. / I had a boss who measured his success by how much Merrill would pay him, how many cars he had, how many homes he had. That's not how I measure my success. Mine's measured by my kids. I look to my kids every day. I've had to do that the last five years while the restaurant isn't making nearly the amount of money I want it to and certainly not what I made on Wall Street.

Are our kids happy? Are they successful? Are they getting opportunities? I think society today is way too materialistic. It is nice to aspire to make money, and it is nice to aspire to have nice things. We had a huge home and a huge kitchen with a Viking refrigerator—but if you don't have your family, you're lost.

I did a lot of multimillion-dollar deals when I worked on Wall Street. I had a lot of fun. But the thing I have been most successful at is coaching a basketball team that I now have time to do. We're 18–0 this year. I think I am teaching these kids how to be successful, how to compete, what you can accomplish with hard work.

K.H. / **Any books or resources you would recommend to others?**
T.S. / Nothing beats real-life experience. Not just on-the-job training, but talking to people who have been in the business. That's your best resource. I talked to people who owned restaurants. I talked to people running sub shops, fast-food restaurants, people who had worked as servers in particular restaurants. I bought a couple of books, but until I was doing it, those didn't help me. Talk to as many people as you can to get real live input.

THE ABCS OF FRANCHISING

For his first two years in the restaurant business, Tim Sheerer was a franchisee of an Italian restaurant chain. It taught him the ropes and gave him the confidence to make the initial change and, eventually, to embark on his own small, family-run eatery.

Not all franchises are created equal, and getting into the game can be expensive. Within the same industry, the more expensive franchises are better known in the marketplace; therefore, they can command a higher price because you are buying into the value of a well-known name. The less expensive franchises may not have any name recognition and are looking to expand their presence in the market by offering their franchises at a much lower price. It is essential that you do your homework and research on a potential franchise to avoid future mishaps.

Careful planning is fundamental to success. The U.S. Small Business Administration (www.sbagov/smallbusinessplanner/start/buyafranchise/index.html) offers resources to help you get started. Here are some guidelines:

WHAT IS FRANCHISING? A franchise is a legal and commercial relationship between the owner of a trademark, service mark, trade name, or advertising symbol and an individual or group wishing to use that identification in a business. The franchise governs the method of conducting business between the two parties. Generally, a franchisee sells goods or services that are supplied by the franchiser or that meet the franchiser's quality standards. The franchiser provides the business expertise (marketing plans, management guidance, financing assistance, site location, training, etc.) that otherwise would not be available to the franchisee. The franchisee brings the entrepreneurial spirit and drive necessary to make the franchise a success.

THE TWO FORMS OF FRANCHISING. These are product/trade name franchising and business format franchising. In the simplest form, a franchiser owns the right to the name or trademark and sells that right to a franchisee. This is known as product/trade name franchising. The more complex form, business format franchising, involves a broader ongoing relationship between the two parties. Business format franchises, such as the one Tim Sheerer was involved with, often provide a full range of services, including site selection, training, product supply, marketing plans, and even assistance in obtaining financing.

BUYING A FRANCHISE. Because of the risk and work involved in starting a new business, many new entrepreneurs choose franchising as an alternative to the risk of starting a new, independent business from scratch. One of the biggest mistakes you can make is to hurry into business, as Tim Sheerer did, so it's important to understand your reasons for going into business and determine whether owning a business is right for you. But remember that hard work, commitment, and sacrifice are essential to the success of any business venture, including franchising.

FRANCHISING TIPS FROM THE
SMALL BUSINESS ASSOCIATION

Here's how to start investigating a particular franchise that interests you:

- Request an information packet from the franchiser.

- Interview owners of current franchises.

- Research the industry and other franchises in this industry.

- Seek expert advice to better understand the franchise agreement.

- Review the costs related to getting into this franchise and compare them to the costs of starting a nonfranchised business in this industry.

Check out these links:

THE AMERICAN FRANCHISEE ASSOCIATION (AFA) (www.franchisee.org) is a national trade association of franchisees and dealers with over seven thousand members.

THE INTERNATIONAL FRANCHISE ASSOCIATION (www.franchise.org), founded in 1960, is a membership organization of franchisers, franchisees, and suppliers.

FROM THE CORPORATE LADDER TO THE PULPIT

▼

After graduating cum laude from the University of Chicago in 1971, Diane Rhodes landed a job with Illinois Bell Telephone Company and moved on to AT&T's New Jersey headquarters in 1979. She made a classic climb up the corporate ladder, juggling managerial duties with earning an MBA. For years, she traveled the country to conduct sales training and speak at industry conferences, addressing up to four hundred listeners at a pop.

When AT&T began trotting out early-retirement packages, Rhodes didn't qualify. In fact, she was busy developing programs to help with downsizing, including job counseling for employees. But she found herself thinking, What might I do if I had the chance?

And then the offer came. "I was proud to work for the corporation, but I had the feeling that maybe I was being called to something else—something more," recalls Rhodes, her blue eyes softening. So at age forty-nine, she snapped up an enticing early-retirement package and withdrew from AT&T's corporate cocoon, a world that had shaped her adult life.

Like many people who retire young, she was badgered by her contemporaries about what was next. She waited. She spent the next year dabbling in administrative jobs at her church. "You really have to take the time to be unsettled until the opportunity presents itself to you," she says. "It's hard to let ourselves live in that tension of the unknown, of not having the questions answered."

Ultimately, Rhodes was led by her faith. She enrolled in a course at Drew University Theological School and began working as an executive assistant to the dean of the seminary. Five years later, she graduated summa cum laude with a master of divinity degree.

In December 2005 Rhodes was ordained an Episcopal priest. "It was a breathless moment," Rhodes says. "Something metaphysically happens." Her first port of call was at St. Andrew's Episcopal Church in Lincoln Park, New Jersey. Then in July 2007 she was named the interim director at St. Andrew's Episcopal Church in Harrington, New Jersey, and she expects more church moves down the road.

Regardless of where she is sent, her salary resides well under $30,000—about a third of her former pay. Luckily, she doesn't fancy sporty cars, designer duds, or deluxe vacations. She prefers to read, do needlepoint, walk, and listen to classical music.

Rhodes is in charge of all the liturgical and spiritual life of the parish. It's a small parish—averaging fifty to sixty worshippers on a Sunday morning. She presides over baptisms, weddings, and funerals, as well as worship services. She regularly visits three nursing homes. "You make eye contact and look beyond into the heart and soul of a person who needs to know that he or she still matters and is a child of God," says Rhodes. She also delivers her sermons to her eighty-nine-year-old mother, who lives in an assisted-living community.

Before leaving AT&T, Rhodes had divorced. Her home was sold and the profits split. She put money down on a condo. Savings from her 401(k) plan plus her pension buyout provide her retirement fund. She has retiree health care coverage, to which she contributes.

The corporate-speaking gigs have given way to heartfelt sermons amid the soaring beams and stained-glass windows of her tiny parish. The audience may be smaller than in her AT&T days, she says, but the spiritual message is deeper.

The hours are still long—more than sixty a week—yet the rhythm is different. Rhodes once caught a train in New York's Penn Station, and a young woman with tears in her eyes saw her white collar and asked to talk. Rhodes paused in her journey to take the time to listen—giving new meaning to the idea of working overtime.

— Q & A —
LOOKING BACK

K.H. / **What did the career transition mean to you personally?**

D.R. / I knew. I had sensed for some time that I was being called in another direction. I did not know at first what it was I wanted to do. But as a person of faith, I have always believed that God issues invitations to us in a number of areas, and we have the freedom to either accept them or not.

I knew there was something going on, that I was being invited to move in a new direction in my life. I just didn't know quite what that was, so when the opportunity came to leave and retire with a package that included health benefits, I just decided it was time to take that risk and do some discernment, and to have the time to do the discernment.

And so I did and began to explore the possibilities of a call to the Episcopal priesthood. I took a few classes at the seminary, and I knew that is where I needed to be. I began the discussion process with my own parish priest and within our diocese. There are rules for that process. I formed a discernment committee who worked with me and prayed with me and was admitted to the ordination process at the Episcopal Church here in the diocese of Newark. I began the seminary part time in 1999, graduated in 2004, was ordained in 2005 in June to the diaconate, and in December to the priesthood.

K.H. / **Did you have any second-guessing? Were you confident you were heading in the right direction?**

D.R. / I think we always second-guess and wonder, and yet I guess I would say second-guessing isn't the word I would use. I would say there are always unanswered questions, and you have to be able to live within the uncertainty of not having things spelled out. The answers aren't there yet. I would call it a leap of faith; someone else might call it a leap of enthusiasm. It's a willingness to go and do something new and different. People experience that in different ways.

K.H. / **Anything you would have done differently?**

D.R. / Not really. I wish I had figured it out a little sooner, but changes like this require time. You can't make them in a hurry. You have to have the time.

K.H. / **What has been the biggest surprise or unexpected reward that has come from this career change?**

D.R. / The absolute delight of working with individuals and congregations. I knew it would be wonderful, but when people invite you to share in the sacred moments of their lives—the happy ones or the ones that are hard, troubling, and sad—it is such a privilege to be invited into that sacred space. And it never fails to fill me with awe, and I am so grateful for that.

K.H. / **How big a role did financial rewards play in your decision to make a career change?**

D.R. / Most clergy don't go into it for the financial rewards. That is not why you choose this vocation. But the income is helpful. My mother lives in an assisted-living community. That's a real part of my financial reality. Her assets are gone, and so in a very loving way that is now my responsibility.

K.H. / **How did your preparation help you succeed?**

D.R. / I took the time to go back to school and pieced it together with partial scholarships. I worked and talked to people who were doing it. I had always been involved for many years as an active layperson in my parish. Out of those ministries came the beginnings, the first stirrings of the fact that I might be called to ordained ministry. Then knowing and working with many fine clergy within our diocese, the idea began to take shape and grow.

"You really have to take the time to be unsettled until the opportunity presents itself to you. It's hard to let ourselves live in that tension of the unknown, of not having the questions answered."

K.H. / **What do you tell others who come to you seeking advice about following their passion or dream?**

D.R. / I serve on our commission on ministry, and I work with people who believe they have a calling. For this vocation, we see it as a three-way call. It is what the person believes they may be called to do. It is also what the community and the church are saying. Is there validation of the call that an individual feels that they may be experiencing? What in their parish life supports that?

That can take a great deal of time. We give people helpful questions to think about: How long have you been thinking about the ministry? What would happen if the church says no? Would you continue to be a faithful person? There are also the nuts and bolts things you need to contemplate if you want to make this kind of career move. Do you accept that there is not a large financial reward? Do you realize that if you are called to be a rector or pastor, you are going to be called to do things like fix the toilet if it breaks? All the wonderful spiritual sides of this life are countered by the realities—and there are chores to do.

K.H. / **How do you measure your success?**

D.R. / That is something I struggle with. It is not something you measure just in terms of how many people attend on Sunday, although that is something that you look at. Our little parish here is growing; I think you feel a growing level of trust and community with the people you serve as well as with the larger diocese. And that is a sign of success. I look at all the opportunities I have had to promote justice and equality within my community and in the larger community. Did I do that? How have I stepped up to this opportunity?

K.H. / **Any books or resources that you turned to?**

D.R. / Aside from the Scriptures? That is a big piece of it. There are always those long, dark nights when you think, have I done the right thing? Is it going to work? You need to find a way to center yourself and create some place of peace amid the uncertainty. For me, I found it between Robert Frost's poetry and the Forty-sixth Psalm.

THE BEST FIELDS FOR STARTING OVER

Some people leap into a second career they've always dreamed about, whether it's opening a boutique or joining a nonprofit group. Others, however, know they're ready for a change but aren't sure what to change into. If you're seeking a more rewarding career but don't know where to look, a good place to start is where jobs are available. These are some of the top job-growth areas where midcareer changers are likely to find work that's both meaningful and challenging:

CLERGY. With widespread worries about the economy, war, and terrorism, it's not surprising that religion is a growth area these days—it's the underpinning of American culture, in many respects. Many clerics spend the bulk of their time ministering to parishioners in their homes. There are, of course, those inspirational sermons from the pulpit, and regular duties like officiating at baptisms and weddings and consoling people in times of grief. Most clergy, despite the image, don't take a vow of poverty: median salary is $78,690, according to Salary.com. Educational requirements vary according to denomination. Many require a graduate degree. Others will admit anyone who is called to the vocation. To learn more, speak to a clergyperson of your faith.

HEALTH CARE. The U.S. Department of Labor lists a variety of home and personal care health care jobs as fast-growing occupations. You don't have to be a surgeon or ICU nurse; there are hundreds of areas of specialization, such as music therapists for autistic children and Alzheimer's patients and occupational therapists for the elderly.

You'll find useful details about health care jobs in the Department of Labor's *Occupational Outlook Handbook* and the

American Medical Association's annual *Health Professions Career and Education Directory*. Other helpful Web sites include Health Professions Network (www.healthpronet.org), which features different allied health professions, and Health Care Workforce (healthcareworkforce.org), which has a long list of links to other job-listing sites in the field.

Given the pressing need for workers, it's not unusual to find streamlined training, including train-while-you-work positions, according to Ellen Freudenheim, author of *The Boomers' Guide to Good Work*. You can also find flexible schedules and opportunities to run your own business, which can be an alluring antidote to the incessant demands of laboring in some huge organizations.

EDUCATION. There's a shortage of teachers from preschool to twelfth grade across the country. If you have a bachelor's degree in any field, you could qualify for an alternative teacher prep program that enables you to begin teaching with salary and benefits within a few months' time. Alternative Routes to Teacher Certification is a free booklet from the U.S. Department of Education. There's also the National Center for Alternative Certification (www.teach-now.org), a clearinghouse for shortcuts to certification funded by the Department of Education.

Be forewarned: helping the next generation blossom can pose challenges in the public school system, where special-ed students and gifted kids sometimes share the same classroom. Teaching at a private school aimed at students with higher-ability levels is an alternative, but it might require more education. There's also a need for tutors and corporate trainers. The median salary for a high school teacher is about $50,000, but there's wiggle room. Go to Salary.com for specific salary ranges by ZIP code.

ELDER CARE. You might already be informally providing this type of help for your own parents—from shopping to cooking meals to offering personal care and companionship. If you're suited to it, there's plenty of need for paid workers at assisted-living homes, memory-care centers for Alzheimer's patients, and traditional nursing homes. Plus, venues for elder care keep multiplying as specialties evolve.

The aging population is also driving up demand for nutritionists, physical therapists, speech and language specialists, and activity aides, who help design programs to encourage socialization and provide entertainment and relaxation.

Patience and a sense of humor are prerequisites, and the work can be repetitive and challenging—sometimes physically. A good place to learn more is the National Family Caregivers Association (www.nfcacares.org).

Pay varies widely, starting in the midtwenties and going much higher. In Philadelphia, for instance, a home care nutritionist might pull in $77,000 annually and a home care chaplain, $55,000.

FROM HIGH TECH TO
HIGH MINDED

John Sage's memories include 1960s antiwar rallies in Berkeley and trailing farmworker activist César Chávez as an eleven-year-old with his socially progressive parents. He also remembers the weekly trip to Peet's Coffee to buy a bag of freshly roasted coffee beans with his father.

For Sage, forty-nine, cofounder of Seattle's Pura Vida Coffee, whose mission is to raise awareness and funding to benefit at-risk children and their families in coffee-growing countries, those recollections are the essence of who he is today.

But Sage mixed in one ingredient all his own: he's a capitalist. "I was the black sheep of the family," he says. "I enjoyed business." As a boy, he ran a lemonade stand and a paper route. In college, he started several businesses to pay tuition. "I was convinced, though, that one day I should entwine being compassionate and being a capitalist."

After graduating from Stanford University in 1983, Sage spent a handful of years working for pharmaceutical giant McKesson, garnered a Harvard MBA in 1989, and achieved financial success as a Microsoft marketing executive. He took a turn as a vice president of a start-up high-tech company, Starwave, which was acquired in 1998 by Disney and Infoseek, leading to his "lucrative exit" as a multimillionaire, he recalls. "I was fortunate to be in high tech at the right time."

The impetus for Sage's transformation was twofold. "First, I found myself at a stage of life where I thought there had to be more. My job was burning me out, and I was hardly seeing my wife and kids. Then I went to a reunion of business-school chums." One was Christopher Dearnley, pastor of a church he'd started in Costa Rica, part of the International Association of Vineyard Churches. He met Sage in San Diego for their annual golfing reunion. Sitting poolside after the outing, Sage was struck by his friend's commitment to his work for the poor, which focused mostly on helping homeless children in the tough neighborhood of Alajuelita.

Dearnley gave his friend a bag of Costa Rican coffee as a present. It hadn't cost much there, but if sold in the United States, was worth three times that amount. "A light went on," says Sage, who had been consulting for Starbucks.

Here was the hands-on, business-driven philanthropy he had been seeking. On cocktail napkins, a business plan for Pura Vida—which means "pure life" in Spanish but in slang translates as "way cool"—began to take shape.

As César Chávez said, "The fight is never about grapes or lettuce. It is always about people." For Sage, it's about people—and first-rate coffee. "It's a great value proposition," he says. "I believe that business can be driven by good, not greed. It takes a tough mind and a tender heart."

Sage supplied over $1 million in start-up money for the new coffee company, with its slogan, "Create Good," and agreed to run operations and marketing from the company's administrative office in Seattle for the first few years. Dearnley would select the coffee suppliers and continue his work in Costa Rica. A portion of net profits from sales and donations would go directly to support social services and provide health care and education programs to growers in Costa Rica and beyond.

In 2009, Pura Vida sold close to one million pounds of shade-grown, organic, certified fair-trade gourmet coffee, meaning that farmers are paid living wages and are guaranteed a fair price. Pura Vida beans are sold over the Web and to student unions and dining halls at more than three hundred colleges. In addition, the coffee is served at thousands of churches across the country, as well as at the House of Representatives cafeteria on Capitol Hill and the Smithsonian Institution's nineteen museums. All told, sales generated roughly $5 million in revenue.

Even better news: to date, the company has distributed over $3 million, including its own contributions, those it encouraged from its distributors, and private donations, which help provide clothes and food to street kids, job training, libraries, computer centers, and scholarships in poor communities in Central America.

Sage's new venture affords him the flexibility that didn't exist in the espresso-fueled, hundred-hour work weeks at Microsoft. He can spend time with his wife and three boys, ages five, eleven, and fourteen, coach baseball, and attend Boy Scout meetings. "I've landed at a great intersection," he says. "In the words of Frederick Buechner, the Presbyterian minister, that's 'the place where your deep gladness and the world's deep hunger meet.'"

— Q & A —
LOOKING BACK

K.H. / **What did the transition mean to you personally?**
J.S. / To me, it represented the integration of those two seemingly disconnected pieces of myself—the idea of being tough-minded and

tenderhearted. On the one hand, I have the desire to compete and to be in the business world and have a front-row seat into a very, very tough business—and at the same time, I want to use those skills as a way to drive social change and promote economic justice. A lot of these things were baked into my upbringing.

For me, it was really a dream. It sounds a little too flowery, but I really felt like there was a validation that there was a way to combine those two things—things that most people said couldn't be woven together.

K.H. / **Were you confident in what you were doing? Any second-guessing along the way?**
J.S. / I had no shortage of confidence, which is generally a good thing. I felt a really strong conviction that the idea of thoughtful consumption seemed to be taking root, and so it feels good to have been on the forefront of that.

K.H. / **Is there anything you would have done differently?**
J.S. / There are a lot of things I would have done differently. I should have put a more demanding set of financial filters and more scrutiny on the basic business model. I was in a position to fund it for several years, which was great, but as an unintended consequence, I didn't really subject myself to the same rigor and discipline that I always talk about. I should have spent some more time really thinking through what it was going to take financially and operationally to scale the business.

I also grossly underestimated how long it would take to support the kind of scale growth that we eventually enjoyed. It was a combination of my optimism and, in part, arrogance—just thinking, how hard could it be? I got an MBA, right? I can do this.

The consequences of that were very significant. I put far more of my own family assets on the line than was wise. And that created strain with my wife. Fortunately, we have worked all that through, and the company is still growing and going.

When I sit down with wide-eyed optimistic social entrepreneurs these days, I sound like I am giving them a dose of harsh news, but it comes out of that experience.

K.H. / **What has been the biggest surprise or unexpected reward for you?**

J.S. / Getting down in the field a couple of times and having a chance to see our programs in operation—it was much more a matter of the heart than of the head. That flipped the switch for me, putting names to some of the families who are directly or indirectly responsible for our product. I draw on those memories and make a point of trying to get out there at least once a year to remind myself why I'm doing this.

I tried to ask people to buy something that not only satisfied a desire, but also offered a karmic benefit. I still think that is a very powerful combination, but I have come to appreciate the power of just asking people to give. When the cause is worthy and merits it and is done in a responsible, effective way, you can just ask for a donation. I think in some instances we've just overcomplicated it.

Another surprise was that I wasn't as strong a business manager as I'd thought I would be. No matter how much goodwill your business engenders, or how well you are connected, or how many people will volunteer and donate their time, the business itself has got to be fundamentally sound, particularly when you are in the commodity business and you are on the wholesale side. You have to have operational excellence when you don't have scale and efficiencies as guys like Starbucks do.

And that also requires that you have leadership and a management team that has a different skill set than I do. I am not a good day-to-day operational, penny-pinching guy. It would have been very helpful to have come to that realization much earlier.

K.H. / **What role did financial rewards play in your decision to make this career move?**

J.S. / None. On the contrary, I eventually drew no salary for six years and had a significant amount of personal capital in the business, which I don't expect to see back. So my overall asset base took a huge hit during that period. There was no expectation at all of any financial return.

▲

"I found myself at a stage of life where I thought there had to be more. My job was burning me out, and I was hardly seeing my wife and kids."

▼

K.H. / **How did your preparation help you succeed?**

J.S. / Perhaps the best preparation was our faith. During a lot of our darkest days and most uncertain times, we would meet and have really great times of spiritual reflection and prayer, usually accompanied by a golf game or two. That was a very important core part of how we coped, how we worked together, and, I think, how we managed to stay such good friends over the years.

K.H. / **What do you tell others who ask your advice about following a passion or a dream?**

J.S. / I try to really encourage them. I hear from people weekly. They are often people who have gotten some of the same criticism I did— that you can't be a successful businessperson and a philanthropist. You can't do that at the same time. Go make your money and then give it away.

I do encourage newcomers and say, "No, you really can weave those strands together." And if done right, they can optimize the outcome of both of those. But I ask very hard, very direct questions to make sure they have thought through the implications and the possible consequences of what they are getting ready to embark on.

I was back at Harvard doing a case study of the company when my favorite professor listened as I described all the great things that were happening—and then he asked, "What about investors?" And I said I didn't really have any because I'd been funding it. And he said, until you have subjected yourself to the rigors of attracting other people's money, all you have is an expensive hobby. It was brutal but true.

K.H. / **How do you measure your success?**

J.S. / I measure it by the fact that the business is still up and running. Despite all the missteps, missed opportunities, and personal failings along the way, there is something in the idea that has attracted attention and taken it beyond my backyard. It's also important to see the impact on the ground.

I look around and see lots of businesses that stand for a double bottom line. They assume that in addition to delivering financial performance, there are going to be social and environmental benefits that spin off as well. It no longer seems crazy, as it was when we started. There's a formation of a capital structure to fund those ventures.

I spend a lot of time lecturing in business schools, and it is very heartening to see MBA students really excited about ideas to launch more businesses like Pura Vida. I had always said that one of the ultimate success factors for me would be to see a new sector of the economy called "for benefit," or whatever. It is nice to see how far it has come.

K.H. / **What books or resources did you find helpful?**

J.S. / David Bornstein's book *How to Change the World: Social Entrepreneurs and the Power of New Ideas*. It came out a couple of years ago. He has written a lot about some of the trends around social enterprise.

I also read a little collection of Martin Luther King Jr. sermons called *Strength to Love*. In particular, there is one sermon in there by the same name in which he really talked about this idea of combining opposites.

WHAT IS A SOCIAL ENTREPRENEUR?

According to Ashoka (see page 186), social entrepreneurs are individuals with innovative solutions to society's most pressing social problems. They are ambitious and persistent, tackling major social issues and offering new ideas for wide-scale change. Rather than leaving societal needs to the government or business sectors, social entrepreneurs find what is not working and solve the problem by changing the system, spreading the solution, and persuading entire societies to take new leaps.

Social entrepreneurs often seem to be possessed by their ideas, committing their lives to changing the direction of their field. They are both visionaries and ultimate realists, concerned with the practical implementation of their vision above all else.

Each social entrepreneur presents ideas that are user friendly, understandable, and ethical and engage widespread support in order to maximize the number of local people who will stand up, seize their idea, and implement it. In other words, every leading social entrepreneur is a mass recruiter of local change makers—a role model proving that citizens who channel their passion into action can do almost anything.

Just as entrepreneurs change the face of business, social entrepreneurs act as the change agents for society, grasping opportunities others miss and improving systems, inventing new approaches, and creating solutions to change society for the better. While a business entrepreneur might create entirely new industries, a social entrepreneur comes up with new solutions to social problems and then implements them on a large scale.

ORGANIZATIONS THAT SUPPORT
SOCIAL ENTREPRENEURS

SKOLL FOUNDATION (www.skollfoundation.org) The Skoll Foundation's mission is to advance systemic change to benefit communities around the world by investing in, connecting, and celebrating social entrepreneurs. The foundation extends its mission through Social Edge, an online resource for the social entrepreneur community.

GLOBAL GIVING (www.globalgiving.com) Global Giving enables individuals and companies to find and support social and economic development projects around the world.

ASHOKA (www.ashoka.org) Since 1981 this organization has elected over two thousand leading social entrepreneurs as Ashoka Fellows, providing them with living stipends, professional support, and access to a global network of peers in more than sixty countries.

SCHWAB FOUNDATION FOR SOCIAL ENTREPRENEURSHIP (www.schwabfound.org) The Schwab Foundation works with Harvard University, Stanford University, and INSEAD to provide scholarship opportunities to the best executive education courses in the field to selected social entrepreneurs.

ECHOING GREEN (www.echogreen.org) Echoing Green invests in and supports outstanding emerging social entrepreneurs to launch new organizations. It offers a two-year fellowship program to help entrepreneurs develop new solutions to society's most difficult problems. Echoing Green sparks social change by providing start-up grants, and supporting and connecting social entrepreneurs and their organizations. To date, Echoing Green has invested $27 million in seed funding to over 450 social entrepreneurs and their innovative organizations.

INVESTORS' CIRCLE (www.investorscircle.net) The Investors' Circle network comprises angel investors, professional venture capitalists, foundations, family offices, and others who are using private capital to promote the transition to a sustainable economy. Since 1992 the Investors' Circle has facilitated the flow of over $130 million into more than two hundred companies and small funds addressing social and environmental issues. Members tend to invest in the following categories: Energy & Environment, Food & Organics, Education & Media, Health & Wellness, and Community & International Development.

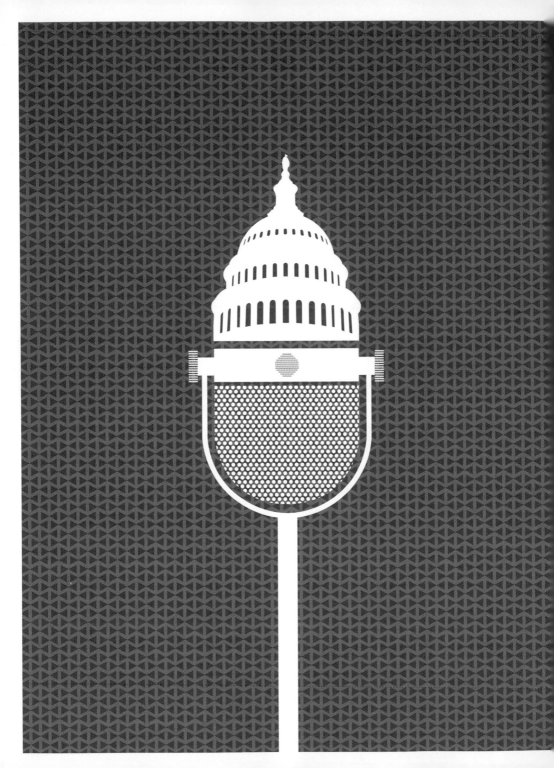

FROM CAPITOL HILL TO CAPITOL HUMOR

It's Saturday night in the Fireplace Room, a classic cabaret setting in Washington, D.C.'s Westin Hotel, and the place is packed with an eager audience of nearly one hundred. They're here to listen and laugh as performer Ken Rynne and pianist and singer Sean Collins take them on a rollicking ride through the latest social issues and political shenanigans in a lively evening of parodies, satire, and song.

The act, performing under the troupe's moniker, Planet Washington, has steadily been drawing in crowds to its au courant show since 2006, and little wonder: it's deliciously fun.

For one-time lawyer, congressional aide, and lobbyist Ken Rynne, fifty-four, "this is living the dream." And though it's little more than a mile from the hallowed halls of Congress—it's an entirely different venue.

Rynne's got the music in him, but it took him twenty-five years to turn it into a career. For the former choirboy, performing has been the thread that has run throughout his entire life. He sang with the Boston Symphony as a fourth grader and around the family television set during Mitch Miller sing-alongs in the sixties.

After graduating from the Boston Latin School, he was awarded a scholarship to go to the prestigious Eastman School of Music but turned it down. "I didn't think music was a serious career," Rynne says. "My dad was a Boston cop, and for some reason, I decided I should be a lawyer."

Rynne studied government at Georgetown University, where he sang with the Chimes, Georgetown's a cappella group. During a college internship in the office of Speaker of the House Tip O'Neill, he contracted "Potomac fever." "It was just fun. Politics and government was the thing," Rynne recalls. After graduation, he continued on to Georgetown University Law Center and then accepted a position practicing energy regulatory law at a D.C. firm.

But seven years later, the practice splintered, and Rynne headed to Capitol Hill to work for Senator Howard Metzenbaum on energy issues. Over the course of seven years, he was Representative Joe Kennedy's legislative director and held staff positions with senate majority leaders George Mitchell, Tom Daschle, and John Kerry. "Every day I felt jazzed, walking through those marble halls," Rynne recalls.

But his toes kept tapping. He wrote and performed in a dozen Hexagon shows—a nonprofit organization that produces an annual musical political satire show performed at the Duke Ellington School of the Arts in Washington, D.C. Rynne also moonlighted with the well-regarded Washington-based troupe the Capitol Steps.

With two young daughters and college tuitions to fund, the time had come to leave the Hill to make some real money. Rynne, like many ex-Hill insiders, signed on as a lobbyist for the American Institute of Architects, followed by a stretch with credit card giant MBNA America in Delaware.

His annual salary ballooned from $35,000 as a Hill staffer to a healthy six figures as a lobbyist. He reveled in the newfound dough, shelling out for a flashy Jaguar to tool around in and buying a McMansion in the suburbs.

But he was lost outside the Capitol Beltway. He found himself drawing up business plans for his own fantasy Washington revue during business meetings, writing musical comedy sketches, and yearning for the spotlight and the laughter. He daydreamed of starting his own show around the theme "Washington, D.C., the musical."

In late 2004 his boss and mentor at MBNA retired, and Rynne knew he needed to break free of the so-called golden handcuffs. "I had been a bit out of place there from the beginning," he says. "I was the proverbial round peg in the square hole. I missed the excitement of Washington politics but wasn't clear on exactly what I should be doing."

The next year, he said farewell to MBNA. Through the firm's human resources department, he learned about Right Management, a consulting firm that specializes in helping executives like Rynne evaluate career options and develop a personal action plan. Through a series of diagnostic tests, they pinpointed two areas that would suit him: education and entertainment.

Bingo. The light went on, Rynne remembers. "That came out as a nice affirmation of where my heart had always been. I decided to move back to D.C. and try the comedy stuff but put a time limit on it." If it did not take off in five years, he would go do what his youngest daughter called "a real job."

Newly single and his daughters now adults, he was free to strike out on a new-fangled path. "I'm in the business of following my heart now," Rynne says.

He sold the big house and car in favor of a rented apartment in Georgetown. And he began to piece together his new enterprise, modeled in part after the Capitol Steps. He set up an LLC corporation, started a Web site, linked up with a mentor, Mark Russell, the master of political satire, and found a collaborator to man the keyboards.

The heart of the show was there. "The writing is easy. It just comes to me. That's the core. Singing, I have been doing forever. That's part of me. That's easy. It's marketing. I had a very naive view of marketing and the nuts and bolts of running the business side."

So Rynne signed up for a community college course to learn how to market a small business. He participated in comedy workshops to hone his material. He reached out to other performers in the city for strategies. And he networked like mad to raise investment capital to get the show on the road and pay for everything from equipment to advertising.

By November 2006 Rynne was ready to hit the stage. He did his first show for an audience of seventy paying patrons. He had the show videotaped to use as a marketing tool when he met with bookers and hotel and restaurant managers to drum up interest. Gradually, he landed a handful of rooms to play, starting with the National Press Club, a natural for his politically savvy act.

But he was naive about show business for a struggling new comedy act. "I had no idea how long it would take to get a cabaret booking. Someone will come in one night, catch the act, and say they want to book us—they're serious, but it can be months before that actually happens," he says. "I thought they would all come running."

Money has been tight. Gigs have come slower than Rynne had expected, but he has hung in there, stretching to meet his monthly budget. With three steady shows each month, he could easily cover his rent and expenses. He boosts his income with consulting projects as a legislative attorney and speechwriting assignments that draw on his political and corporate experience and writing abilities.

As his time in the spotlight swells, Rynne has mastered the art of self-promotion. He smoothly uses his social networking contacts on Facebook and LinkedIn to drum up enthusiasm for his show and build his audiences. He regularly keeps all who know him up-to-date on his appearances and earnestly asks for feedback on the performances to help him sharpen the show. The effort is working. Ticket sales and new dates are climbing.

And he's confident the big break is coming. "Business keeps growing," says Rynne with a wide smile. "I'm happy. I'm living the life. Who needs a Jag when you can have laughter?"

— Q&A —
LOOKING BACK

K.H. / What were you going through personally at the time of the transition?

K.R. / I wasn't very happy working at the bank but was caught up in making the money. Soon I had trouble even going to work. It was hard work to get there. Let me put it this way: they gave me an alarm clock as a gag gift when I left MBNA.

Now the hardest work is filling the room with people. I love writing and performing on stage. I'm in the zone when I'm on stage. People react to me. Everyone gets it. I love it. I write at night, writing at two in the morning. I am working all the time, but it doesn't feel like work.

K.H. / Were you confident and certain in what you were doing? Any second-guessing?

K.R. / I feel certain about my decision today coming off a successful show this weekend. But not always. About a month ago, when I was looking at my financial situation, I started wondering. I have some doubts, but they are purely financial. At this point, I'm in it. I don't want to say, what if? I want to push this thing as far as it goes.

K.H. / **Anything you would have done differently?**
K.R. / From a technical angle, I incorporated as an LLC. I thought it was important to have a business entity for all this money that was coming in. It was expensive to do, and there are a lot of reporting requirements. There was probably an easier way to do it.

I wouldn't have been so naive. I'm not a businessperson. I'm creative. I should have managed my money better to have more saved for the start-up period. But I think I am pretty much where I am supposed to be. I only wish I had done it sooner!

"I'm happy. I'm living the life. Who needs a Jag when you can have laughter?"

K.H. / **How big a role did financial rewards play in your decision?**
K.R. / I'm not independently wealthy, so I need money to pay the bills. But I am not expecting to get a Jaguar again.

K.H. / **How did your preparation help?**
K.R. / I probably should have done more. It started as a daydream, and I thought about it for a long time, fantasized about it, visualized it, and wrote a plan. But then I had to get off the stool and start doing it, and that was harder than I'd thought it would be. Keeping a day job while I got rolling would have provided less financial stress.

K.H. / **Any books or resources that helped you start your second act?**

K.R. / The personality and career diagnostic tests from Right Management helped me focus and know I was heading in the right direction.

K.H. / **How do you measure your success?**

K.R. / My metrics are laughter and applause. Laugher is tough to get. I know I'm fine if I'm paying the bills. It will be great to be in a position where I have to choose between gigs. "Sorry. I am doing the president's dinner that night . . . can't be in Boston."

K.H. / **What are some of the unexpected surprises? Rewards?**

K.R. / Having my mentor, political satirist Mark Russell, laugh at my stuff. He recently sent me a note and referred to me as "a colleague." I graduated from being an apprentice to being a colleague. That's validation—something we comedians always need.

K.H. / **What advice do you give to others who ask you for help in following their passions or their dreams?**

K.R. / I ask them a few simple questions: What do you want to do? What would you rather be doing? Know anybody making money at that? What do they say?

To thine own self be true. Do what you love and the money will follow. I have that saying framed and hanging on my office wall.

KEY THINGS TO CONTEMPLATE BEFORE MAKING
A MAJOR CAREER CHANGE

MARKETING 101 How good are you at selling yourself? Really? This is a key ingredient for those of you embarking on an entrepreneurial second act. This is a genuine blind spot that wannabe second acters can possess.

You may have had a wonderful initial experience starting a new business or a consulting business but fail to understand that your confidence is only part of the battle; the other part is marketing yourself as you move along from those heady first few months or even years. For people who have worked in a setting where they did their job and delivered the end result to much fanfare, this change can be extremely difficult.

GREENHORN BLUES It's much tougher than you think to cope with being a beginner. It's unnerving. You feel as though the rug has been pulled out from under you, and your base of support and confidence has slipped away. To have a second act hit, you must be sufficiently open to change in your life. Career changers often underestimate what the transition will bring and how many things they actually appreciate in their lives. All of a sudden, they realize how they miss their old career or the trappings of it, and they are not really open to replacing those things.

RESPECT We all like to be treated with respect. We enjoy the admiration, esteem, and appreciation we get from colleagues, people we manage at our current jobs, our bosses, and others whom we come into contact with both socially and professionally. We take pleasure when those around us have a high opinion of us.

But when you move into uncharted territory, you're a neophyte, the proverbial new kid on the block, starting over at the bottom. This requires some psychological adjustment and fine-tuning. All of a sudden, you are making less, probably making a few mistakes, and not being treated like the experienced professional you have come to be.

LOOK INSIDE AND RECOGNIZE THOSE FEELINGS You might even want to hire a professional such as a therapist or career coach to guide you through this more personal adjustment. A supportive partner or best friend might be all the shoring up you need, but it is a transition phase that shouldn't be ignored.

MAKING MISTAKES GRACEFULLY Easier said than done. Face it, the older you are and further along on your professional success ladder, the harder it is to accept criticism and responsibility for screwing up. Your ego just isn't as nimble and forgiving as it once was. This is the reality, and it happens when you start anew. When you're in your twenties, you are better equipped to handle the inevitable screw-ups and missteps, let them slide off your back with a simple shrug, and move on.

When you can accept that trying new things means learning from your mistakes along the way, you will be in a healthier, stronger place to move ahead. Doing things badly is just another step toward doing them well.

AFTERWORD

Changing your work life can be risky, but as you've seen from the people you met in these pages, it can be a successful risk—and, even more so, a truly satisfying one.

If you've lost your job and are dealing with a second act as a necessity, it's crucial that you don't act out of rashness and fear but, rather, knowledge of how you can use this life-changing event to your advantage. True, you may not have the luxury of savings socked away to tide you over while you gain traction in your new work. And you may not have a limitless time horizon before you need to start earning enough to support you and your family.

But, in reality, this may very well be the perfect time to move into a job that means something to you. With the cushion provided by a severance or early-retirement package, grab hold of your chance to try something you have always dreamed of doing, even if it isn't on your timetable but your ex-employer's whim.

We all wrestle with just what it is we're looking for in our job and life. How many times have you been told that life is short and not to waste it? To make a complete turn, though, usually takes spirit, strength, and a thirst to find meaning in this life. Not everyone is hardwired for that kind of transformation.

If you've finished this book with a gnawing sense of excitement in your belly for the possibilities out there, you most certainly are one of the lucky ones.

No two paths are the same. Each person I interviewed was faced with a different set of challenges. But these success stories do reveal common threads.

Many of these men and women were spurred to discover what really matters to them and transform their work (and, in turn, personal) lives by a crisis or loss that starkly revealed the fleeting nature of a life. No one acted impulsively. They paused. They planned. They bypassed helter-skelter approaches and pursued prudent, well-researched moves.

Each person set flexible time horizons for his or her venture to make it. If necessary, these people added the essential skills and degrees before they made the leap. They often apprenticed or volunteered beforehand. They reached out to their networks of social and professional contacts to ask for help and guidance.

They downsized and planned their financial lives in order to be able to afford a cut in pay or the cost of a start-up. Several were fortunate to have had the cushion of a spouse's steady income or had some outside investments, retirement savings, and pensions in place to ease the transition to their new line of work.

But what really sticks with me is that they all share a clear confidence in the direction they have taken. They collectively work longer hours, but it doesn't matter. They only wish they had done it sooner.

And that says it all.

Good luck!

IDEAS FOR FURTHER READING

DON'T RETIRE, REWIRE by Jeri Sedlar and Rick Miners / Alpha, 2002 Sedlar and Miners focus on people who are already retired and are looking for work situations that are mentally and emotionally rewarding—whether it's a part-time job, volunteer work, or a second career. The authors have come up with some fresh approaches to self-exploration.

ENCORE: FINDING WORK THAT MATTERS IN THE SECOND HALF OF LIFE by Marc Freedman / Public Affairs, 2007 Freedman is the founder and CEO of the think tank Civic Ventures and cofounder of Experience Corps, the nation's largest nonprofit national service program for Americans over fifty-five. His book is a guide for people who want to build a better world through their work. Freedman provides concrete steps to finding a meaningful new job and profiles encore careerists.

ESCAPE FROM CORPORATE AMERICA: A PRACTICAL GUIDE TO CREATING THE CAREER OF YOUR DREAMS by Pamela Skillings / Ballantine Books, 2008 Skillings writes about toxic workplace issues such as bullying bosses, hapless coworkers, incurable boredom, and widespread racism and sexism. She provides a multitude of questionnaires, exercises, and worksheets to help determine a dream job, assess expenses and assets, and plot an escape plan to break free of corporate life without going bust. In addition to giving advice on where and how to find career coaches, health insurance, and jobs, Skillings shares some people stories.

ESCAPE FROM CUBICLE NATION: FROM CORPORATE PRISONER TO THRIVING ENTREPRENEUR by Pamela Slim / Portfolio, 2009 Life coach Slim shows readers how to navigate the transition from corporate worker bee to entrepreneur.

HOW TO CHANGE THE WORLD: SOCIAL ENTREPRENEURS AND THE POWER OF NEW IDEAS by David Bornstein / Oxford University Press, 2004 This has become the bible for social entrepreneurship. It profiles men and women from around the world who have found innovative solutions to a wide variety of social and economic problems.

LOOKING FORWARD: AN OPTIMIST'S GUIDE TO RETIREMENT by Ellen Freudenheim / Stewart, Tabori & Chang, 2004 Freudenheim tells readers how to successfully pursue everything from second careers to additional academic degrees to volunteer work.

SMART WOMEN DON'T RETIRE—THEY BREAK FREE by the Transition Network and Gail Rentsch / Springboard Press, 2008 Here's a practical guide for boomer women searching for what's next.

TEST-DRIVE YOUR DREAM JOB by Brian Kurth / Business Plus, 2008 The founder of VocationVacations offers a guide to finding mentors and your own dream job.

THE THIRD CHAPTER: PASSION, RISK, AND ADVENTURE IN THE 25 YEARS AFTER 50 by Sara Lawrence-Lightfoot / Farrar, Straus and Giroux, 2009 The author approaches this stage of life from her perspective as a sociologist. The book's premise is that life's third chapter is one of substantial growth and change.

WHAT COLOR IS YOUR PARACHUTE? 2009: A PRACTICAL MANUAL FOR JOB-HUNTERS AND CAREER-CHANGERS by Richard Nelson Bolles / Ten Speed Press, 2008 This handbook for job seekers of all ages and skill levels has been a classic for more than three decades.

WHAT SHOULD I DO WITH MY LIFE? by Po Bronson / Ballantine, 2005 Fifty inspiring profiles of those searching for their true calling.

HELPFUL WEB SITES

NONPROFITS

BOARDNETUSA.ORG is for those interested in board service.

BRIDGESTAR.ORG lists senior positions in nonprofit organizations.

COUNCILOFNONPROFITS.ORG links local nonprofits across the country through state associations.

ENCORE.ORG lists nonprofit job opportunities.

GUIDESTAR.ORG is a leading source on nonprofit organizations.

IDEALIST.ORG leads to more than fourteen thousand volunteer opportunities nationwide, plus internships and jobs in the nonprofit sector.

INDEPENDENTSECTOR.ORG offers research and resources of over six hundred charities, foundations, corporations, and individuals.

PHILANTHROPY.COM/JOBS lists jobs primarily in foundations.

FOR JOB SEEKERS

AARP.ORG lists workplaces that are particularly friendly to aging boomers.

BOOMERSNEXTSTEPS.COM connects experienced executives with short- and long-term management positions.

CAREERBUILDER.COM is an extensive overall career site.

CAREERONESTOP.ORG offers career resources to job seekers.

CAREERPATH.COM is a broad resource site with a variety of tests to help identify career paths.

DINOSAUR-EXCHANGE.COM lists short- and long-term job opportunities for retirees.

ENCORE.ORG offers help in searching for a career with greater meaning.

EXECSEARCHES.COM connects experienced nonprofit, government, education, and health workers with executive, midlevel, and fundraising positions.

EXECUNET.COM connects executives with recruiters.

EXPERIENCECORPS.ORG is geared to Americans over fifty-five who want to tutor and mentor in underserved schools.

MONSTER.COM lists large general jobs with a special section for older workers.

RETIREDBRAINS.COM offers nationwide job listings searchable by industry or state.

RETIREEWORKFORCE.COM lists job postings and offers résumé services.

RETIREMENTJOBS.COM verifies employers offering a friendly work environment for older workers.

SENIORS4HIRE.ORG is where seniors can apply for jobs, submit a résumé, or post a description of their model job.

WHATSNEXT.COM is a broad site with a range of resources from finding a career coach to quizzes and other practical tools.

WORKFORCE50.COM lists jobs exclusively from employers who are keen about hiring workers over age fifty.

YOURENCORE.COM connects retired scientists, engineers, and product developers with consulting and short-term assignments.

CONTINUING EDUCATION

FASTWEB.COM is a search engine for research scholarships and grants for older students offered by associations, colleges, religious groups, and foundations.

IRS.GOV offers information about educational tax breaks.

NASFAA.ORG offers a wide range of college resources, from financial aid to ways to save and pay for school.

STUDENTAID.ED.GOV offers federal financial aid to offset education costs (no age limit to apply; part-time students eligible).

SMALL BUSINESSES

ALLBUSINESS.COM is an online media group that offers resources, including business forms, contracts and agreements, expert advice, and more.

KIVA.ORG lends funds worldwide to entrepreneurs.

LENDINGCLUB.COM is a financial community that connects borrowers and lenders.

PROSPER.COM matches borrowers and lenders typically looking for small loans (a few thousand dollars).

SBA.ORG offers complete small-business resources, from loans to franchising to tips on starting a small company, from the U.S. Small Business Administration (SBA).

SCORE.ORG is a nonprofit association dedicated to educating entrepreneurs and the formation, growth, and success of small businesses nationwide.

STARTUPNATION.COM is a site dedicated to small-business groups.

ZOPA.COM partners with a nonprofit credit union with over 61,000 members worldwide.

NETWORKING

FACEBOOK.COM has over 300 million users and is a place to connect with friends and businesses.

LINKEDIN.COM is a professional social network.

THETRANSITIONNETWORK.ORG is a virtual community for women over fifty.

XING.COM is one of Europe's leading social and professional networks.

VOLUNTEERING

1-800-VOLUNTEER.ORG is a database of nationwide projects.

LAWYERSWITHOUTBORDERS.ORG directs legal pro bono services around the world.

ONLINEVOLUNTEERING.ORG is a database sponsored by the United Nations to help find online volunteering opportunities with organizations that serve communities in developing countries.

OPERATIONHOPE.ORG seeks volunteers with a background in the financial industry to work as virtual volunteers to victims of hurricanes and other disasters, offering financial and budget counseling via the Internet.

VOLUNTEER.GOV is a one-stop shop for public service volunteer projects sponsored by the U.S. government.

VOLUNTEERMATCH.ORG allows you to search more than fifty-four thousand listings nationwide. Its extensive database of projects lets you screen for everything from board opportunities to communications positions based on your interests and geographical location.

TAPROOTFOUNDATION.ORG places teams of professionals who are doing pro bono consulting with nonprofits. Operates in seven U.S. cities in a variety of fields, including finance, marketing, and information technology.

FUNDRAISING

AFPNET.ORG The Association of Fundraising Professionals represents over twenty-six thousand members in 171 chapters throughout the United States, Canada, Mexico, and China, working to advance philanthropy through training courses, advocacy, research, education, and certification programs.

FOUNDATIONCENTER.ORG The Foundation Center educates thousands of people each year through a full curriculum of training courses—in the classroom and online. Free and affordable classes nationwide cover grant-proposal writing and fundraising skills. The group operates library/learning centers in five locations—New York City, Washington, D.C., Atlanta, Cleveland, and San Francisco—that offer free access to information resources and educational programs.

CAREER COACHES

ACPINTERNATIONAL.COM Association of Career Professionals.

CERTIFIEDCOACH.ORG The International Association of Coaching has a searchable list of certified members.

COACHFEDERATION.ORG Nonprofit organization source for those seeking a coach. Referral service links with more than thirteen thousand professional personal and business coaches.

COACHU.COM Since 1992, this outfit has offered extensive coach training programs. Findacoach.com, one of its services, provides a searchable database of over two thousand coaches by type of coaching and fees.

NCDA.ORG The National Career Development Association has an extensive state-by-state database to find a counselor, plus links to career planning sites to guide you to self-assessment tools to salary information and more.

PARW.COM Professional Association of Writers and Career Coaches— source for finding a certified professional résumé writer, interview professional, and career coach. The CPCC credential is awarded to those members who have completed the association's extensive training program.

WABCCOACHES.COM Worldwide Association of Business Coaches.

FRANCHISING

AAFD.ORG The American Association of Franchisees and Dealers is a national nonprofit trade association that offers educational programs, resources, and more.

FRANCHISE.ORG The International Franchise Association is a membership organization of franchisers, franchisees, and suppliers.

FRANCHISEE.ORG The American Franchisee Association (AFA) is a national trade association of franchisees and dealers with over seven thousand members.

SBA.GOV This site of the U.S. Small Business Administration features a small-business planner section.

SOCIAL ENTREPRENEURS

ASHOKA.ORG Ashoka Fellows are provided with living stipends, professional support, and access to a global network of peers in more than sixty countries.

ECHOINGGREEN.ORG offers a two-year fellowship program to help entrepreneurs develop new solutions to society's most difficult problems.

GLOBALGIVING.COM enables individuals and companies to find and support social and economic development projects around the world.

INVESTORSCIRCLE.NET comprises angel investors, professional venture capitalists, foundations, and others who are investing private capital into companies and small funds addressing social and environmental issues.

SCHWABFOUND.ORG The Schwab Foundation for Social Entrepreneurship works with Harvard University, Stanford University, and INSEAD to provide scholarship opportunities to the best executive education courses in the field to selected social entrepreneurs.

SKOLLFOUNDATION.ORG has a mission to advance systemic change to benefit communities around the world by investing in, connecting, and celebrating social entrepreneurs.

ACKNOWLEDGMENTS

I am indebted to so many people for their contributions, support, and wisdom:

I am most grateful to my "second acters," who shared their stories, inspiration, and precious time with me. You're making a difference not only in your own lives but in others' journeys as well. I am in awe.

To the career experts who were always there to take a phone call or respond to an e-mail to point me in the right direction—Marc Freedman, Betsy Werley, and Beverly Jones—I am beholden.

The Second Acts column, which has appeared in *U.S. News & World Report* since 2006, would not have become a reality without the vision and skilled editorial touch of *U.S. News & World Report* Executive Editor Tim Smart. Thanks, Tim, for giving me the opportunity to run with this concept and meet these remarkable individuals. In addition, the careful shaping and shepherding of the profiles on to the printed page in each issue lay in the magical wordsmith hands of James Bock and James Pethokoukis.

If not for my brother, Mike Hannon, who recruited my first two career changers from his deep network of friends and colleagues to recount their successful career changes in my hometown of Pittsburgh, Pennsylvania, this path into second careers might never have taken flight. Mike, thanks for having my back.

My appreciation to my agent, Linda Konner, whose enthusiasm and insight made it possible for this book to be published.

My admiration to my editor, Ursula Cary, who knew immediately the magic of helping people follow their dreams and deftly wove together a book that motivates and educates with panache.

As always, I prevailed on my husband, Cliff, to critique my drafts, and he cheerfully and thoughtfully never hesitated to do so. Thank you.

To the entire Bonney family—Paul, Pat, Christine, Mike, Caitlin, and Shannon—for always carrying me under your wing and allowing me to share in those blissful days at Villa Hakuna Matata in St. John, where I started working on this book.

To Jane Kelso, who opened the doors to the joys of Rappahannock County and the creative forces that propelled my days of writing there amidst the quiet and mountain vistas.

To my trainer, Jonelle Mullen Stern, and the crew at TuDane Farm, who offered me respite from deadlines atop a horse cantering down to jumps, or roaming along pine-needle trails.

To my brother, Jack, who is always there when I need him.

Lastly, to my mother, who never fails to encourage me and listen, and to my late father, John W. Hannon, who always nourished my dreams. You were right: You do have to dream to get there.

And, of course, to Zena.

INDEX

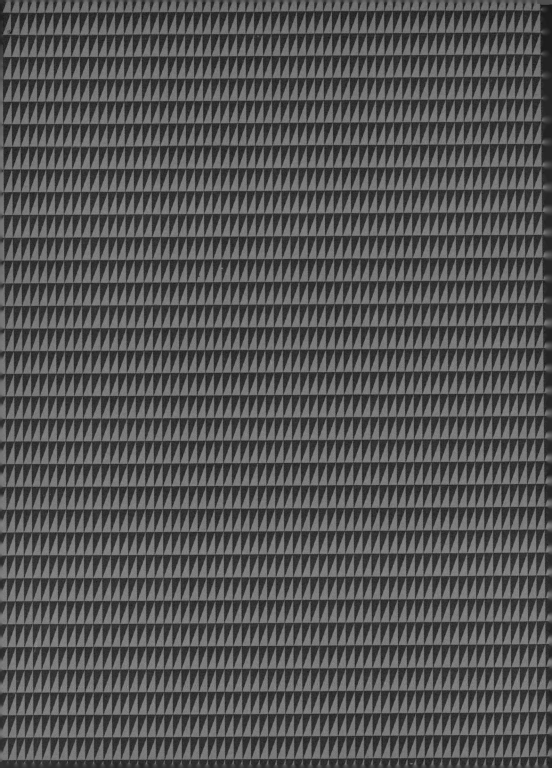